PRAISE FOR *THEIR SECOND WORLD WAR*

I am delighted this book has been written to educate children about World War II – it is really important to ensure the sacrifices of this generation are never forgotten.

Her Majesty Queen Camilla

This excellent book could not come at a more appropriate time, and should be widely read by the younger generation.

Dame Joanna Lumley

Victoria Panton Bacon's collection of Second World War memories for children is history brought to life. With infectious enthusiasm she transports the reader into people's homes as if they were visiting friends or family. She sits us at people's tables or on their sofas so that we can hear first-hand how it felt to be a sailor or an airman under fire, or a townie child evacuated into the care of countryfolk in Devon, or how a young Jewish girl found ways to endure the cruelty of her Nazi captors.

Victoria gives us proper adventure stories that ring true and bridge the gap between today's young people and a rapidly disappearing generation today's youngsters will be proud to claim as their models and heroes.

Ian Whybrow
Author of more than 100 children's books,
translated into 27 languages, including
the Harry and the Bucketful of Dinosaurs series

This is a fascinating and important collection of authentic memories, skilfully distilled and curated by Victoria Panton Bacon, and with haunting, tender illustrations by Kerry Timewell. It should be in every school to ensure these stories are never forgotten.

James Mayhew
Author and illustrator of more than 60 books for children, including the Katie series and *Once Upon a Tune*

Victoria focuses on hope, on liberation, on the smallest details, but without ever trying to step clear of the darkness.

Joshua Levine
Second World War Historian and author of
Dunkirk: The History Behind the Major Motion Picture

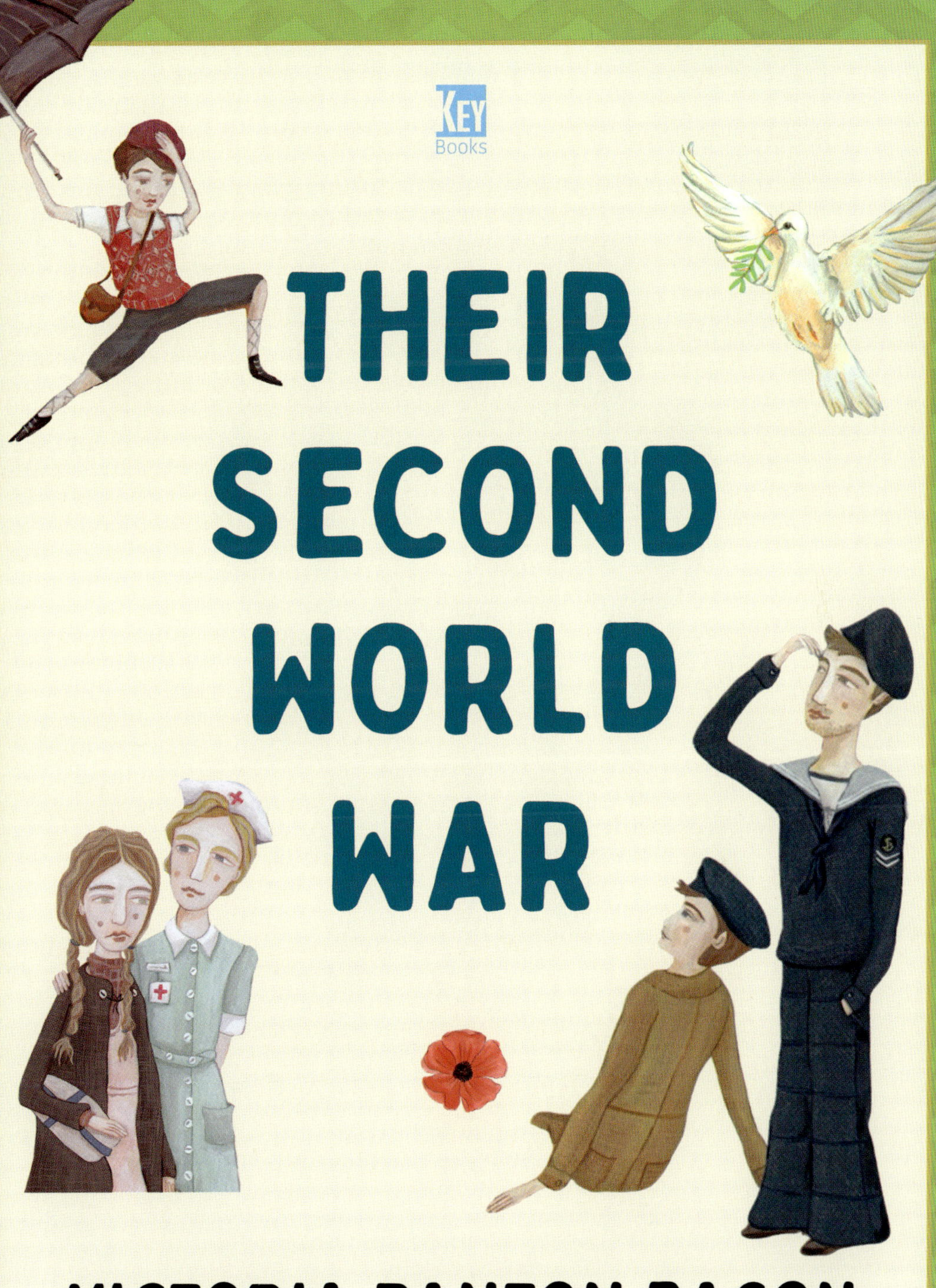

THEIR SECOND WORLD WAR

VICTORIA PANTON BACON

Illustrated by Kerry Timewell

A special thank you to the wonderful team at The History Press, who have published two of my previous works, *Remarkable Journeys of the Second World War* and *Remarkable Women of the Second World War*. Several of the stories in *Their Second World War* are drawn from these books, written in full for adults, and Key Books and I are proud to bring these special and vital recollections to a younger audience.

I would also like to thank the veterans who have recalled their memories — and the family members who have encouraged them to do so, bringing this book to life. Thank you also to the wonderful team at Key Publishing for your enthusiasm, and hard work in presenting this so beautifully — Francesca Studholme-Smith, Simona Hill and Myriam Bell. Thank you also to Sarah Baxter at the Society of Authors and Emma Shercliff for your guidance, and to Christopher Hand for proofreading.

Thank you, too, to all those who have kindly supported this book with your warm words of endorsement — Her Majesty Queen Camilla, Dame Joanna Lumley, Ian Whybrow, Joshua Levine and James Mayhew. A huge thank you, of course, to Kerry Timewell for her lovely illustrations, and — last but not least — to my husband William and children Rollo and Ranulph, who have listened to every chapter as the words have been written and who understand just how much this book means to me, and have supported me every step of the way.

Finally, thank you to all the readers of *Their Second World War*. By reading it you are caring for what was given. Thank you all!

~ Victoria ~

Published by Key Books
An imprint of Key Publishing Ltd
PO Box 100
Stamford
Lincs
PE9 1XQ

www.keypublishing.com

The right of Victoria Panton Bacon to be identified as the author of this book has been asserted in accordance with the Copyright, Designs and Patents Act 1988 Sections 77 and 78.

ISBN 978 1 83632 093 7

Images used on pages 19, 25, 28, 30, 31, 37, 38, 41, 47, 49, 54, 59, 66, 69, 73, 81, 88, 110, 114, 123, 124: Alamy

CONTENTS

FOREWORD

As I write, I can't help feeling sad that the Second World War is fast fading from living memory. There are very few people alive to tell us what that astonishing period was really like. Before living memories turn to history, their voices must be recorded – and Victoria Panton Bacon has done that in a particularly important way: she has made them accessible to, and understandable for, children.

When I was young, this period loomed much larger in our collective social consciousness than it does today. When somebody spoke of 'the war' or 'the last war', their meaning was clear. And while it was almost a legal requirement for my friends and I to make Spitfire models, we were also keen to make models of other great Royal Air Force aeroplanes too, such as Boulton Paul Defiants and Gloster Gladiators. I realise, now that I am older, how important it was that I made these models; they may only be 'plastic toys' but they helped me learn about the war, and develop an interest in these vital years. A yearning to know as much as I can about it that has never gone away. Things have changed. It would be odd if they hadn't. But we must not lose what is important along with the plastic toys. What matters is our understanding of world history and who we are within it.

So much of what we take for granted nowadays came directly out of this period; for example, the huge scale of illness and injury during the Second World War led to the rapid development of medicines such as antibiotics, and military computers developed during the war have undoubtedly contributed towards the growth of technology, which continues to this day.

We must never forget how many of our modern benefits and advantages were hard-won during the darkest years of the conflict. And we must be able to recognise the warning signs when today's decision-makers send out clear echoes of past behaviours.

How, though, to introduce the period to children? This, I believe, is where Victoria has truly excelled. She has set out the experiences of people like us – and she has done it in the most vivid and relatable way. Ivor Foster was a Lancaster gunner whose heated flying suit failed at 21,000 feet. In this book, he explains calmly and clearly how this felt and why he had no choice but to get on with his job. What could possibly be more vivid?

And how do we explain the Holocaust to children? How do we explain something that surpasses any person's understanding? Victoria tells the story of Mady Gerrard, an inmate of Auschwitz and Belsen. She focuses on hope, on liberation, on the smallest details – but without ever trying to step clear of the darkness. You will not quickly forget the story of how, in Belsen, Mady learned to make necklaces from beads found on electrical wires, and how she traded these beads for food with the German women in charge.

We are in real danger of forgetting all these things.

Victoria will help us to remember. Make no mistake about it – this is an important book.

Joshua Levine,
November 2022
Second World Historian and author of the *Forgotten Voices of the Blitz and the Battle for Britain* series and *Dunkirk: The History Behind the Major Motion Picture*

WORLD WAR TWO KEY DATES

JANUARY 1933 — Adolf Hitler and his followers, called the Nazi Party, gain control over Germany. Hitler wishes to expand German rule across Europe.

1 SEPTEMBER 1939 — Hitler invades Poland.

3 SEPTEMBER 1939 — France and Britain declare war on Germany.

30 MAY 1940 — Winston Churchill becomes Prime Minister of Britain.

22 JUNE 1940 — France surrenders to Germany, after a brutal invasion.

10 JULY 1940 — Germany launches an air attack on Britain. These attacks last until the end of October and are known as the 'Battle of Britain'.

6 JUNE 1944 — The 'Allied' forces (Britain, France, The United States and The Soviet Union) landed on beaches in Normandy, known as the D-Day landings, to push 'Axis' forces (Germany, Italy and Japan) out of France.

7 MAY 1945 — Germany surrenders to the Allies.

2 SEPTEMBER 1945 — Japan surrenders to the Allies, marking the official end of World War Two.

INTRODUCTION

What do you think of first when someone asks you about the Second World War? Bombs? Aeroplanes? Rows of buildings damaged in the Blitz? Warships battling the high seas? Wounded men, lying in beds in makeshift hospitals? Evacuee children carrying their gasmasks in small rectangular bags over their shoulders? Perhaps you think of the British Prime Minister, Winston Churchill, smoking his trademark cigar?

The stories in this book are all true memories, gathered from testimony given to me by those who lived through the war. The recollections do recall much of what you might expect in a book about the Second World War, but there is much here that, I promise, will surprise and enlighten you and, I hope, leave you yearning with a quest for much greater knowledge. Each story has been honestly told and written to broaden your knowledge about what it was like for so many people, from different walks of life, who lived through the Second World War – and to enable better understanding of these vital years.

By *knowing* about the war years, we can understand (at least a little bit) and by *understanding* we will *remember* this war. These years of our history are now passing from living memory, so capturing as much of the truth as we can from those who lived through it is very important. Each of the men and women who have recalled their wartime memory for this book represent so many more. For example, Pat Twyman, who missed her home and family so terribly as an evacuee at the start of the war, tells her own story; but the homesickness and fear she describes was, of course, felt by so many children. Ivor Foster, in recounting his memory of being part of an immense fleet of aircraft taking part in a bombing raid over Germany, tells his story for the thousands of others who also flew in such raids. Mady Gerrard's heart-wrenching reflection of the Holocaust, too, sadly, was experienced by thousands of others.

It is a privilege for me to have received these precious memories; but the stories were not given to me so only I would know of them. Each was given to me so that I would take the trouble to write it, share it, take the memory forward; so that the remarkable men and women featured in this book will be remembered, as will their friends, comrades and loved ones, too.

These men and women opened their hearts and minds so that you might know what was given, endured, and lived through between 1939 and 1945. Without such immense courage, resilience, and determination we may have lost the war and life for us, now, would certainly be very different.

We have so much to be grateful for. We have a duty to understand what was given during the Second World War and there is no better way to understand than to learn of the war through the words of those who were there. Thank you all for the memories!

Victoria Panton Bacon

CHAPTER ONE

IVOR FOSTER

LADY LUCK - AN AIR GUNNER'S STORY...

A gigantic flying carpet

How often, perhaps when you are playing in your garden or at the beach, have you heard the roar of an aircraft engine and turned your head to the sky to look for it? It is quite thrilling, isn't it, if you do spot it, to watch it going in and out of the clouds and wonder momentarily where it is going to, and where it came from, before it disappears. Imagine, now, if you saw several aircraft altogether flying neatly in formation (such as the Red Arrows, for example, the Royal Air Force's [RAF] aerobatic team – nine aircraft take part in its displays). Nine aircraft in the sky together would (I think!) be nine times more exciting than seeing only one.

This is where it gets trickier, because I am going to ask you to imagine something almost *unimaginable*. But just before I tell you

what that is, I need to remind you that this book contains *only* true memories of the Second World War. So, what I am going to ask you, in a moment, to imagine – did happen. Now, back to your imagination.

Imagine the roaring rumble of an aircraft engine in your head and look up to the sky. However, you don't just see one aircraft, or nine, or 19, or 90, or even 900. You see more than 1,000 aircraft – not small ones, either. Above you are more than 1,000 of the RAF's largest, four-engine bombers, the mighty Lancaster, each one with a wing-span more than 100-feet wide – that is roughly the same length as a blue whale! Imagine seeing nothing above you except a dark mass of deafening aviation brilliance such as this, screaming across the sky, a carpet of aircraft encapsulating the courage of more than 7,000 men.

The most memorable day…

Ivor Foster told me about being part of one such raid. He was one of 7,000 men, in the same part of the sky, at the same time. Ivor Foster ('Blondie' was his nickname, because he was the only blond man in the crew) was a mid-upper gunner on the RAF's largest heavy bomber aircraft, the Lancaster, which had a crew of seven. He was one of the Lanc's two gunners; as mid-upper gunner, he would have been seated in a perspex (a solid, transparent plastic) turret, poking out of the top of the aircraft's fuselage (the body of the plane); the other gunner was the rear gunner (meaning he was seated at the back).

Each member of the crew had a different and equally important job: the pilot (naturally!) flew the aircraft; a navigator plotted the course it would take; a wireless operator communicated with ground crew; an air bomber released the bombs; and a flight engineer was responsible for the maintenance of the aircraft (in the air and on the ground). When they were on a raid, all were exposed to flak (that is anti-aircraft fire, blasted at them by enemy guns) and attack from enemy aircraft, but the two crew members most exposed were the gunners, because of their position outside the main body of the aircraft. They were called gunners because they had large guns, with lots of ammunition pointing out of their turrets, which they would use to blast gunfire at the enemy when they needed to – at the same time telling the pilot what was happening around them so, if he could, he would fly the aircraft away from danger.

Ivor Foster's aircraft was part of a formation raid, as described above. Known as '1,000 Bomber Raids', the one he told me about took place on 11 March 1945, over Essen, Germany. Essen was one of a number of German cities (others included Dresden, Cologne, Berlin and Hamburg) that Allied commanders defined as areas to be 'strategically attacked' because these were the cities housing the largest bomb- and rocket-making factories, so needed to be destroyed. Railway stations and marshalling yards that facilitated the enemy's ability to keep up their campaign were also targeted.

It was Ivor Foster's Wing Commander who delivered the 'battle order' to Ivor's RAF Squadron (186) just hours before departure for this raid. Ivor recalled that every spare crew and aircraft were pulled into service. He said he has never forgotten hearing the words of the order which were: 'The target for this afternoon, gentlemen, is Essen. The effort will be maximum, using over a thousand bombers: one thousand and seventy-nine, to be precise.'

We set off in the sunshine. We were in a group of 149 Lancasters, known as the Daylight Group. We left our base of Stradishall in Norfolk, and then circled over Southampton, in a 'V' formation. We were at about 22,000 feet, the first 'group' of all the aircraft to get to Southampton.

Then the other 900 aircraft arrived, and I remember Jack (the bomb aimer, sitting in the 'nose' of the aircraft), saying through our intercom 'here they come!' and I looked over the side and couldn't see the ground, there were so many planes. Those bombers went off ahead of us because they had visual targets to strike, whereas we were attacking using radar*, so we went behind them; more than one thousand pilots pointing the noses of their aircraft in the same direction, first towards France, and then Germany.

---

* The type of 'radar' deployed on this operation was known as 'window' radar. The idea was that metal strips of paper (hundreds of them would need to be dropped in one go) falling into an enemy area would confuse the enemy, because the metal would be attracted to its radar system, overwhelming it with false 'echoes', causing false alarms.

The 1,079 aircraft were made up of 750 Lancasters, 293 Halifaxes and 36 Mosquitoes. It was the second largest RAF raid of the war, only surpassed the next day by an even bigger (the largest of the entire war) raid on Dortmund.

A chilly moment

The flight described above was possibly the most remarkable of the 16 operations Ivor Foster completed during the Second World War, but it was not the day on which he was most terrified.

Day number one, for sheer terror, was during his training. This is quite an amazing story, not least because it is also about the friendship nurtured within his crew, so important for young men so far from home, taking part – day after day – in precarious operations for which they knew there was a possibility, every time, they may not return.

This is the brief story of a gunner (Ivor) and his pilot (Philip Gray) and it is about something that happened during a training flight, while they were stationed at Woolfox Lodge in Leicestershire. It was 19 December 1944. Winter was in its icy grip, but by this time the Lancaster crew had bonded (the same crew stuck together until the end of the war), and no matter what the air temperature was, their growing friendships – as described to me by Ivor – always gave them a 'warm' glow. Ivor spoke to me, particularly, of the respect he had for Philip Gray ('we couldn't have been blessed with a better pilot', he said), respect that didn't diminish on this cold, cold December night. This is what happened:

Our instructions that evening were to fly from Woolfox Lodge to Land's End and back, with five other Lancasters. The weather was appalling, absolutely dreadful, but Phil decided to complete the trip, regardless; the only one of the six Lanc pilots to do so. For the whole time we were met with cloud – cumulus nimbus – everywhere, upward currents throwing downward currents – for six hours, in complete darkness, because we didn't set off until 7pm.

Ivor told me the outside temperature when their aircraft reached 21,000 feet was -47 degrees Fahrenheit; so cold that even the

heaters in the body of the aircraft began to cool down, and so cold that both the gunners – Ivor in his turret at the top of the aircraft and Clyn, the rear-gunner at the back – plugged their flying suits into the aircraft's electrical system; something they would have done only when it was dangerously cold. 'But', said Ivor 'that was the night my suit 'went for a burton' (a wartime expression for going missing). The electricity cut out shortly after he turned it on, and once again Ivor was cold – very, very cold. He needed (and wanted so much) to simply retreat from his turret (in which he felt as though he was turning into a block of ice…) and clamber into the cockpit and share Philip's heater. But that escape was not to be. Philip reminded Ivor of the importance of his position by saying:

THIS IS AN RAF RECRUITMENT POSTER FROM WORLD WAR TWO. THE AVERAGE AGE OF PILOTS DURING THIS TIME WAS ONLY 20 YEARS OLD.

'Up there you have the best view of all the action, and right now I need all the help I can get. A shout from you in time might just save our necks.' So, Ivor remained in his turret for the duration of this whole flight – six hours of icy chill, endless impenetrable cloud, bitter cold, snow, sleet and electrical storms – followed by one of the most difficult landings, for Philip Gray, of his career.

I asked Ivor how he felt about being told to 'stay put', even though he was genuinely at risk of freezing to death. 'Surely you were annoyed with Philip for that?' The response was an emphatic 'No! Philip had a whole crew to think about. I just had to put up with it... and what better training could there be?'

Ivor had one more memory to share with me – this one about the importance of 'Lady Luck':

Lady Luck was with us on every flight. If she hadn't been, we wouldn't have come home. Phil said to us, after every safe landing, 'Lady Luck's been with us again.'

Now I am 95 years old, and I think of 'Lady Luck' every day. I was with a fantastic crew during the war and was very sorry when we were all posted to different stations after the end of the war in August 1945. But Lady Luck stayed with me – I had a long and happy marriage with my dear wife Bearnice; and I've had three careers; the RAF, the police, and finally I looked after adults with mental illnesses.

Thank you, Lady Luck!

CHAPTER TWO

DOUGLAS HUKE

ON THE HIGH SEAS IN THE MERCHANT NAVY

All aboard!

'Something amazing happened – the Aurora Borealis – I saw the Northern Lights! It was really wonderful!' Douglas Huke's excitement at seeing this display of green and blue shimmering light hardly seems to have diminished, even though almost 80 years had passed since then when he told me this story.

Douglas Huke experienced the magnificence of the 'midnight sun' – as the Northern Lights are also known – in May 1940, while serving in the Merchant Navy, as a wine and bathroom steward on board His Majesty's Ship (HMS) *Ormonde*. At the time, the ship was anchored in Scapa Flow in Orkney, on the way to Norway to collect troops and prisoners of war. Aside from the glory of the lights (for which many people these days pay good money and travel specially to see) it was an otherwise challenging and difficult trip for *Ormonde* and its crew. They were in a convoy of Royal and Merchant Navy vessels sent to Norway because the Germans had invaded there a few weeks before. When Douglas and his crew arrived, the campaign was reaching its intensity during which, he told me, the enemy continued to mount a very strong defence. He said, 'German ships came on to us all night, even though we had the cruisers HMS *Sheffield* and *Ark Royal* as our escorts. A tanker, an armed trawler and HMS *Orama* were shot and torpedoed. Nineteen of *Orama*'s crew drowned; the rest, including the captain, were taken prisoner.'

This memory is important, too, because it tells us of the peril of the torpedo. Torpedoes were underwater missiles, blasted towards the hull of an opposing vessel from a submarine (the Germans called them U-boats – *Unterseeboot*) that would often simply lie in watery wait for its prey. The Allies had plenty of torpedoes attached to submarines too; and for both sides it proved to be a terrifyingly destructive and effective weapon. After the war, Prime Minister Winston Churchill wrote, 'The only thing that really frightened me during the war was the U-boat peril', particularly referring to the Battle of the Atlantic, (which was the longest continual military campaign of the Second World War, lasting throughout the whole of the conflict). This was a hugely decisive battle, which the Allies eventually won. The Atlantic was a vital route used throughout the war by the British and Americans for transporting men, food, weapons and fuel. If the enemy had

managed to block this lifeline, the outcome of the war might have been very different. However, despite being victorious, it cost the Royal and Merchant navies dearly; around 80,000 men succumbed to the ocean's cold, grey, salty water.

Anyone for a cuppa?

Douglas Huke's journey to Norway is one of many trips he undertook between 1939 and 1945; he served in the Merchant Navy throughout the whole of the war. This chapter is a story of 'journeys within a journey' because, as one of the 185,000 seamen who served in the Merchant Navy during the Second World War, he was constantly on the move. Sometimes he sailed quite peacefully on calm waters – but often, he told me, conditions would be scarily tempestuous – so much so that Douglas's description of how *Ormonde* would often lurch in the wind made my stomach churn, and I felt chilled to the bone when he told me how cold and wet he would sometimes get when he was stuck outside on deck duty.

The real Aurora Borealis.

WINSTON CHURCHILL

* He was born on 30 November 1874 and died on 24 January 1965.

* He was Prime Minister TWICE! Firstly from 1940–1945, then again from 1951–1955.

* He was known for his rallying speeches, which helped the British public to feel brave and determined, even on the darkest of days.

* Some of Churchill's most famous quotes are:

'I have nothing to offer but blood, toil, tears and sweat'

'We shall fight on the beaches, we shall fight on the landing grounds…we shall never surrender'

'Let us therefore brace ourselves to our duties… [so that] men will say, "This was their finest hour".'

However, that said, the memory that follows is a warm and sunny one. Enjoy! The date is 3 September 1939. Is this date ringing a bell? It is the date that Prime Minister Neville Chamberlain declared we were at war with Germany.

The news that the Second World War had begun didn't reach Douglas, however, until quite late in the day because he was on-board HMS *Ormonde*; having joined the Merchant Navy six months before the war began. On this day, he was already on his way to Australia, for the second time. The crew was told that war had been declared, just after docking in Colombo, the capital of Sri Lanka. Immediately, conditions for *Ormonde*'s 1,650 crew members changed, because they then fell under the orders of the Royal Navy.

'We were ordered, straightaway, to black out all our port-holes', Douglas told me, 'then we were allowed to go exploring – the weather was really warm and it was all so pretty. There was lots of tea for sale, and we all bought some – lots of it – we spent what little money we had on lovely tea, to take back home!'

For this journey, after leaving England, *Ormonde* had first taken its crew to Gibraltar, then into the Mediterranean passing France and Italy, before sailing to Port Said in Egypt and Oran in Algeria, where they 'bunkered' for a while, and where *Ormonde* was refuelled. Colombo was the staging post after Oran; and then – replete with tea and sunshine – the crew continued to Australia; Cockatoo Island in Sydney Harbour to be precise, which is where hundreds of British and colonial convicts were imprisoned in the mid-19th century.

Bang! BANG! BANG!
(and bunny rabbits…)

It was in Sri Lanka that I thought I was going to lose me hearin! We had no passengers at the time and the captain suddenly said, 'Well, we've got a gun, so we're going to fire the gun!' And he did, and it was so loud it shook the poor old ship to kingdom come! She was a 1906 ship, she couldn't take it, I thought she was going to fall to pieces. But after that he threatened to shoot another one – the first one was a 6-inch gun that had been fitted to the 'aft deck', and the second one was going to be a 3.5-inch*

---

*   An 'aft deck' is the deck located at the rear of a boat or ship.

FACT FILE

A merchant navy is made up of commercial and trading ships, and their crews.

In 1939, Britain's merchant fleet was the largest in the world.

Merchant shipping was greatly needed in wartime, to carry servicemen overseas to fight, and to carry the supplies to equip and sustain those fighting men.

Approximately 185,000 seamen, including 40,000 men of Indian, Chinese and other nationalities, served in the British Merchant Navy during the war.

The life-line is firm thanks to the MERCHANT NAVY

anti-aircraft gun, fitted to the promenade deck. It was only when one of the crew pointed out to the captain that if he did let it go again, we'd probably lose one, or even both, of our funnels; and he held back. Thank goodness he did!

The next part of the voyage was quite bizarre and, I suspect, required a good sense of humour just to get through it. On arrival in Australia, Douglas recalled picking up a few passengers, but the only cargo they took on board were crates of skinned rabbits, which they stored in the ship's freezer. He said they offered the rabbits to everyone they met at the ports they stopped at on the way home, including in the Philippines, Algiers and Malta, but nobody wanted them. He said, 'We only managed to get rid of the damn rabbits when we eventually arrived back home, in Tilbury Docks!'

A sea-service of which to be proud

Douglas Huke's Continuous Certificate of Discharge lists 15 engagements between April 1939 and June 1945, after which he had to take sick leave, finally leaving the Merchant Navy in October 1945. During the war he covered thousands of sea miles, sometimes to the East, to Australia twice, America, Africa and often into Europe. Being on board a troop ship, he met and helped hundreds of troops, and hundreds of prisoners.

A German U-boat.

He was able to recall some of his journeys in far greater detail than others. Not surprisingly the distances, places, miles and memories of his travels have become confused – they have merged into an ocean of their own. During his years in the navy, Douglas was always on the move too, and no two days were ever the same. Life 'on the ocean wave' was, undoubtedly, very hard indeed, but one that was as fulfilling as it was fearful, full of surprises, camaraderie, and pain – both mental and physical.

Sadly, the Merchant Navy lost more than 30,000 men during the war; a death rate proportionately higher than any of the other armed forces, most of whom were drowned while on board the 1,550 merchant ships that were targeted and overcome by the enemy. However, their contribution will be remembered with gratitude. Below are the words of the Right Honourable Alfred Barnes MP, Minister of War Transport, delivered to the House of Commons in October 1945:

The Merchant Seaman never faltered. To him we owe our preservation and our very lives. The thanks of this House be accorded to the officers and men of the Merchant Navy for the steadfastness with which they maintained our stocks of food and materials; for their services in transporting men and munitions to all the battles over all the seas, and for the gallantry with which, though a civilian service, they met and fought the constant attacks of the enemy.

The Red Duster …

Officially known as the Red Ensign, the 'Red Duster' is the flag of the Merchant Navy, created for the Royal Navy in the 17th century, but adopted many years later by the British merchant fleet. It is a bright, cheery red flag with a Union Jack in the top left-hand corner. Long may it fly, for Douglas and his Merchant Navy shipmates, who bravely conquered the ocean waves so we could have our freedom.

A World War Two poster, supporting the Merchant Navy.

CHAPTER THREE

PAT TWYMAN

A LONG WAY FROM HOME

'Hello Patricia…'

'Mum!'

When this surprise phone call took place, Patricia (Pat, as she will be for the rest of this chapter) Twyman was only ten years old – and had not heard her mother's voice for nearly two months. Young Pat had been evacuated from her home in Gravesend in the southeast of England to Totnes, 189 miles away in the southwest; and since the day she left home – at the beginning of June 1940 – Pat hadn't spoken to her mother at all.

'I never answered the telephone at the house I was staying in; I never really thought I should. But that day I happened to be standing next to it when it rang so I just picked it up. I couldn't believe it was my Mum.'

Despite Totnes being a quaint seaside town, and it was summer too, so probably making it all the prettier, Pat did not have a very

happy time at her evacuee home. However, she said at the time she was 'accepting of the circumstances', living in the present, keeping herself as busy as she could and not thinking of her family in Gravesend too much. But when she heard her mother's voice, she said, 'I suddenly realised how terribly home-sick I actually was, and I told Mum I wanted to come home. I pleaded with her, and it wasn't difficult to persuade her to make arrangements for me to come back because not much had happened in Gravesend, so they weren't too worried about my being unsafe there.'

When Pat left Gravesend, in Kent, to begin her evacuee adventure, she departed with many other children, some of whom – like Pat – had never spent a single night away from home. A few children, I expect, may have been quite excited, but most, I think, would have been confused and deeply upset by the sudden separation from their parents, made so much harder by not knowing at all when, or even if, they would be re-united.

Pat and her friends were among 1.5 million children evacuated from cities to the countryside during the Second World War; children whose lives were turned upside down because it was decreed by the government that they should be away from the dangers of bombing that were likely to be more prevalent in cities, particularly London, than in the country. The process of adjustment for all was enormous; first and foremost, for the children themselves – young children like Pat – but also for the

FACT FILE

* The first mass evacuation, known as Operation *Pied Piper*, began in Britain on 1 September 1939, the day Germany invaded Poland.

* Each child carried a gas mask and wore a label giving the name of the place they were traveling to in case they got lost.

* Sometimes the evacuees were assigned a family to live with. In other cases, people from the countryside came and chose the children they would take with them.

country families that suddenly expanded, and for the mothers, fathers and grandparents left behind.

It hardly bears thinking of, does it? So many families divided and missing each other. It was difficult for parents and children to keep in contact too; not all homes had landline telephones and there wasn't a postal system as we have today – certainly no emails or mobile phones! Pat told me that what surprised her most about answering the telephone to her mother was the realisation that her parents knew how to contact her. Up until then, she had thought they probably didn't even know where she was.

Pat Twyman, who is 92 as this is written, has never forgotten the moment she was put on the train, even though the journey took place more than 80 years ago. She remembers how frightened she was; she, and all the children, were too young to understand why they were being sent away to unknown places, with unknown people. I hope that they were able to draw a little bit of comfort from the fact that, on the train, they were surrounded by other children, almost all of whom would have been feeling the same sense of displacement.

DID YOU KNOW?

PARENTS WERE ISSUED WITH A LIST DETAILING WHAT THEIR CHILDREN SHOULD TAKE WITH THEM WHEN EVACUATED. THESE ITEMS INCLUDED A GAS MASK IN A CASE, A CHANGE OF UNDERCLOTHES, NIGHT CLOTHES, SLIPPERS, SPARE STOCKINGS OR SOCKS, TOOTHBRUSH, COMB, TOWEL, SOAP, FACE CLOTH, HANDKERCHIEFS AND A WARM COAT.

A POSTER FROM WORLD
WAR TWO, PROMOTING
EVACUATION.
LEAVE THIS TO US
SONNY — YOU OUGHT
TO BE OUT OF LONDON
MINISTRY OF HEALTH EVACUATION SCHEME

FACT FILE

* An air raid shelter was a protected structure, often underground, designed to shield civilians and military personnel from bombing attacks.

* According to a 1940 survey, 9% of people slept in public shelters and 4% slept in underground railway stations, 60% of people were on duty at night or just slept in their own homes, and 27% of people used an 'Anderson shelter'.

* The Anderson shelter was named after Sir John Anderson, who was placed in charge of air raid precautions.

* They were free to people who earned less than £250 a year, or could be bought for £7. They were buried about one metre into the ground and could hold up to six people.

* In total, around 3.6 million Anderson shelters were built, and these days, some have been dug up and are used as sheds!

It was, Pat recalled, a long and exhausting journey; after leaving London, the train soon reached the comparative peace of the countryside. For the first time she saw the undulating hills and terrain of Hampshire, followed by Wiltshire, Dorset and Somerset and finally their destination county of Devon. If they had continued, they would have reached Cornwall, and England's most western peninsula; after which there is nothing but the Atlantic Ocean between us and the United States of America.

Pat then told me how she and Kathleen were met at Totnes station by an austere lady who had agreed to take them in, as evacuees, at her home. Upon meeting her, the young girls were invited to address the lady, their 'evacuee mother', as Mrs K. She took them straight to their 'new' home, which was a large house, with a large garden, about five miles from the town of Totnes. It had two staircases: one for Mrs K, and another for everyone else.

Kathleen and I shared a bedroom; it was quite comfy. But we didn't feel very welcome. Mrs K had a son who was about our age, but he didn't like us being there much. He was missing one of his hands, so had a stump instead at the end of one of his wrists and he used it to hit us. Mrs K had quite a lot of money. Mr K wasn't there because he was away, serving in the Royal Air Force.

From what I can remember, Mrs K didn't get out of bed very much. She had a maid who looked after us and did almost everything. When we didn't have to go to school, Mrs K would give us two shillings and sixpence and tell us to go and 'lose ourselves'. Kathleen and I would go into Totnes and buy Maltesers.

Another girl, even younger than me, was staying at the house as an evacuee, too, but I don't remember seeing very much of her. The three of us went to the same school, in Totnes. I remember that Kathleen and I had to walk there and back, but this little girl had a taxi. I don't know why we weren't allowed to share it! So, we ended up hitch-hiking — often we'd be picked up by soldiers in their lorries. That was fun.

It was not long after the surprise phone call with her mother, however, that Pat did return to Gravesend. Kathleen's mother arrived to collect them both, and after packing their few belongings and saying a hasty goodbye to Mrs K, the children left leafy Devon, with much relief, to return to the familiarity of their home county of Kent.

There is no doubt Gravesend was far more of a target for bombing than Totnes. It was only about 30 miles from the centre of London and felt the 'heat' of the Battle of Britain in 1940. Gravesend was targeted because of its factories, some of which manufactured essential war items including anti-aircraft guns, fuel-tanks for aircraft and gas masks. It also had a large airport, which was the base for 35 RAF squadrons.

Pat recalled the reassuring presence of the airmen when they would come into Gravesend on their time off; indeed, some of her happiest memories of the war were of time spent in their local pub with her

Children wearing gas masks.

parents and other families. She said they all really enjoyed it when the RAF men arrived, because they would talk about their flights and operations, and about the aircraft. 'And', Pat said, 'they always had lots of sweets!'

A huge number of incendiary bombs were dropped over Kent during the war, more than in any other part of the country. These were not bombs that exploded on impact, but they were equally dangerous because they were designed, instead, to catch fire. These were frightening enough but, Pat told me that what she – and her mother especially – were most frightened of were the Doodlebugs*.

'I do remember one especially terrifying day, when my Mum was hanging up the washing in the garden, and she saw a Doodlebug, which she thought was coming towards her. Luckily it struck a barrage balloon** on its way down, so didn't do a huge amount of damage, but my poor Mum, she was so scared. I've never seen her run into our air-raid shelter so fast.'

This was a scary memory to recall, but I am glad Pat's recollection of this moment jogged her memory to tell me about

---

* Doodlebugs were rocket-shaped bombs with 'wings' that flew through the air extremely fast. The Germans deployed them during the last few months of the war, firing most of them at central London and Kent. They killed more than 5,400 people and caused a vast amount of damage.

** Barrage balloons were large (about 62 x 25ft [19 x 7.5m] in diameter). They were oval and tethered to the ground with strong wire cables. Some were suspended in the air up to 5,000 feet high, pushing enemy bombers higher into the sky; but their main purpose was to lessen the impact of a rocket coming towards the ground. They were mostly positioned in industrial areas and ports – hence why they were a familiar sight in Gravesend.

their family air-raid shelter; because she said how proud she was of her mother who managed to make it comfortable, cosy and even warm with a little fire – and neither was it dull to be in because they had books and games, and lamps to light it, so it wasn't dark.

Finally, I know much of this chapter is about Pat's mother, but her father – of whom she was equally proud – needs to be remembered too. He served in the Home Guard during the war as he was (just) too old for front-line service. So, as well as protecting local civilians in whatever way he needed to, he spent most of the war guarding enemy targets, such as the factories described above, which was the main duty of Home Guard troops in that area.

'The war was very busy for my father,' she said, 'I didn't see much of him because he was always out. But, as a child, I was probably luckier than most because after I came home from Devon at least I got to see both of my parents every day.

That was my Second World War.'

CHAPTER FOUR

PETER BLACKBURN

A NAUGHTY HOME GUARD RECRUIT

'Can we get there, and back, before the old man sees us?'

Peter Blackburn was 14 years old and at Culford School in Suffolk when, in early 1940, he saw a German Junkers Ju-88 aircraft falling to the ground. It had circled in the sky for a few minutes after being shot at by an Allied plane, then spiralled down. Peter told me how he and his friends watched the skirmish and then the aircraft crash-landed on the other side of a large lake, outside of their school grounds.

A few days later, the temptation for Peter and his friends to see the fallen aircraft for themselves was too hard to resist; they knew going out-of-bounds was forbidden, but this was something he described as an adventure that simply *had* to be undertaken. He told me about the unfolding incident:

We stood there, watching it, and as we did so it began to turn. The pilot must have seen the large house (that was our school building); for safety we all ran inside pretty quick and immediately the air-raid siren went, and everybody rushed down to the cellars.

We learned afterwards that the German had used his bombs elsewhere, but he machine-gunned the house, and most of the bullets went into the headmaster's study. Anyway, Allied planes appeared and shot him down, and he landed the other side of the lake. This lake went right through the grounds of our school, and we used to go fishing there, and sometimes walk along the bank. However, we weren't allowed

A real Junkers Ju 88.

to go across to the other side, over the bridge, without special permission. But we did, and we liked it because there was a lot of wildlife, a tremendous variety of birds, because much of the lake had reeds and there were warblers and other types of birds, coots, water hens. We'd enjoy that.

So, the Junkers was shot down and landed the other side of the lake. We could see some of the wreck from our school. On a Sunday afternoon, very soon afterwards, a rumour went around that we could get to it by going over the bridge. So, lots of us went to see it and we ripped pieces off it. I tore a piece off the swastika*, gathered up machine gun bullets,

---

* A symbol in the form of a black bent cross, used as the emblem of the Nazi party.

and other things. Some of the boys took oxygen cylinders; you name it, we took it.

Then suddenly, one of the boys said, 'The old man's coming', and Doctor Skinner, our headmaster, was coming towards us _ not looking very happy. Some of us hid behind trees, but most of us were caught.

Peter and his friends went to bed with sore backsides that evening (being hit with a cane as a form of punishment was legal in those days), but they did not regret their adventure. It was perhaps a young person's way of finding out a little more about the enemy; naughty, unarguably, but how much these boys would have learned that day; and what a lot they would have had to talk about. And goodness knows they wouldn't have been alone with their curiosity – exploration like this, by young and old, I expect would have been happening the world over.

Curiosity continued...

Peter Blackburn developed an insatiable appetite to know about what was happening in the world around him. From the moment the Second World War was announced by

NEVILLE CHAMBERLAIN

* He was born on 18 March 1869 and died on 9 November 1940.

* He was the Prime Minister of the United Kingdom from 1937 to 1940.

* Chamberlain wanted to keep peace with Nazi Germany, and in 1938 attempted to make an agreement with Hitler that would prevent war from breaking out. This was known as the Munich Agreement.

* In March 1939, Hitler broke the agreement and by September, Britain and France decided to declare war against Germany.

Prime Minister Neville Chamberlain, on 3 September 1939, Peter did whatever he could to gather information, including listening to the radio and reading newspapers in the school library. He also recorded some of the discoveries he found the most interesting in small red diaries that he shared with me. Below are three of his entries; little did he know his scribbles would make it into a book, some 80 years later!

Monday 29th January 1941 – No change in Libya and Eritrea. Italian fighter shot down by Greeks. London had a lot of incendiary bombs. 2 Jus [Junkers] shot down on Norfolk coast.

Wednesday 31st January 1941 – Enjabara (Ethiopia) captured, and Abyssinian revolt rapidly growing in strength because Dangila was captured. 300 prisoners captured in Albania. Minesweeper HMS Huntley reported lost. Strong force of Australians disembarked in Singapore to augment the garrison in the colony.

Thursday 1st February 1941 – South African troops captured important town of Mega in Abyssinia, taking 600 prisoners (mostly European) and guns. Mega is an air base. The Greeks reported capture of two villages with 300 prisoners and 50 guns. Large formation of bombers and fighters attacked Berat, in Albania.

Time for action

At last, Peter Blackburn reached the age when he could leave school. He didn't dislike Culford, especially, but it wasn't where he wanted to be after the war started; he wanted to play his part in the war effort. He came from a farming family in Norfolk, and after leaving school he helped out on the farm while eagerly learning everything he could about what was happening in the war. As soon as he turned 17 on 20 May 1943, he signed up to join the Pulham Market Home Guard; proudly its youngest, and quite possibly, I expect, its most enthusiastic, member.

The main role of the Home Guard, originally called the Local Defence Volunteers because its members were all unpaid, was to act as a 'secondary' defence force to those on the front line; most importantly to be on hand in the event of a German invasion. In this regard, Peter took his role very seriously; because his branch of the Home Guard was in Norfolk and not far from the sea, it was an especially vulnerable area.

Peter was one of around 1.5 million men and women who joined the Home Guard between July 1940 and December 1944, which was when it was operational. Members were all part-time and British citizens, either too old or too sick to join front-line services – or were working in what were known as 'reserved occupations', for example, doctors, teachers and farmers (Peter's father was a farmer, so he stayed at home) – basically, all those working in important skilled jobs, needed for the survival of the country.

In addition to receiving first aid training, home guard troops took part in drilling exercises; Peter completed no less than 87 drills during his service, often on chilly Sunday mornings. Troops were also taught about how to look after people if there was a gas attack; bomb disposal; anti-aircraft warfare; map-reading; and about coastal artillery. Peter was able, too, to sharpen up his shooting skills, which he was particularly pleased to do. Being a farmer's son, he'd learnt to shoot from a young age, encouraged to do so by his father to keep the number of pestilent rabbits (and other vermin) down; it was something he thoroughly enjoyed.

He told me, 'In those days with the number of rats and rabbits it was normal to have guns – rifles and shot guns. In the Home Guard we did a lot of practise shooting using Lewis guns, as well as Stens, .303s and other rifles. I was able to hold my own in shooting, so I was often in the team to shoot against other home guard units.'

But even so, he said he was rather alarmed when – shortly after signing up – he was told that in the event of invasion, and 'meeting the enemy', he could / should use a bayonet* – which

____

* a blade that may be fixed to the muzzle of a rifle and used to stab an opponent in hand-to-hand fighting.

meant they could stab, but not shoot. He said, 'We were instructed that no prisoners were to be taken, and we should use a bayonet as we were short of ammunition. I had, by this time, shot many rabbits but I couldn't have stuck a bayonet into a bunny, let alone a human being standing in front of me. I am sure I would have come off second best – can you imagine that, as a 17-year-old farm boy?'

Wartime skies in East Anglia

The Home Guard may have been a secondary defence force, and the invasion for which the East Anglian troops feared did not materialise, but that did not mean all its residents were shielded

Winston Churchill inspects members of
the Home Guard in 1941.

from the war taking place in the world around them. Many young men and women left its towns and villages to serve on the front line. Inevitably, many did not come back. The grief of those left behind was a sadness being shared the world over.

Also, in this part of England, a picture of war was painted in the sky in a way unlike any other part of the country. This is because, in the east of England, there were many American air bases – home during the war to around 50,000 US 8th Army Air Force personnel – flying and / or maintaining hundreds of enormous four-engine American aircraft, including the B-17 Flying Fortress and the B-24 Liberator, each of which had crews of ten men. At times, huge numbers of these vast aircraft would take to the sky at the same time. Peter recalled: 'You wouldn't believe it today, how many planes there would be in the sky at once. When the Americans went out on their daylight missions there were lots of B17s and B24s in the air at the same time. Crashes were frequent, both when they were going out and when the damaged planes returned to base.'

Next time you hear an aircraft roaring across the sky, take a moment to think how very much louder that sound would be if it were multiplied by 100… and don't be surprised that Peter Blackburn, now no longer with us, remembered that sight and sound, until the day he died.

CHAPTER FIVE

CAPTAIN PARFITT

AN INFANTRYMAN'S STORY OF OPERATION OVERLORD

Some are born lucky

Thankfully, Captain Parfitt didn't spend too long in the mortuary where he was taken, presumed dead, after being struck by shells and mortar while serving as an infantryman during the Normandy Landings, in France, in June 1944.

D-Day happened on 6 June 1944; when the (ultimately victorious) long-planned, highly secret and enormous Allied operation to free France from four years of German occupation finally began. Success was essential; if the Allies had failed, the outcome of the war would almost certainly have been very different. A decision was taken by world leaders including British Prime Minister Winston Churchill and President Roosevelt in North America, shortly after the US entered the war in late

1941, that France – and other countries that had been taken by Germany earlier in the war – had to be liberated, no matter what. The leaders knew, of course, from the beginning that this was far from a straightforward objective; and not for a moment was the manpower required underestimated.

Indeed, Operation *Overlord* (which was the Allied code-name for D-Day and Normandy Landings) was hugely extensive. Before the invasion was launched, more than two million troops from all three services (the Army, Royal Navy and RAF) and from 12 countries (though most were British, Canadian or American) gathered in Britain, in preparation; trained as best they could be for the frightening and unpredictable battle that would take place on the other side of the Channel.

So it was that thousands of young men, Allied servicemen, arrived in northern France on 6 June 1944, initially landing on five beaches along the 50-mile stretch of coast that had been identified as the first area that needed to be taken back. The beaches were, from west to east: Utah, Omaha, Gold, Juno and Sword.

Utah and Omaha were where the Americans were to land, Juno was the beach attributed to the Canadians, and Gold and Sword were the British beaches. Sword was the landing point for Captain Parfitt. Aged 27, he was one of around 150 young men of a similar age, proudly serving in the 1st Battalion of the Royal Norfolk Regiment. They, in turn, were part of a much wider infantry (foot soldiers) unit known as the 3rd Infantry Division, which included – among other units – soldiers from the Royal Warwickshire Regiment and the Shropshire Light Infantry.

KERRY.J 2022

Allied soldiers wade through the sea as they approach the Normandy beaches in 1944.

The weather, by all reports, was foul for the time of year – cold and windy. The conditions in the west were the most challenging, but Sword too was miserably chilly and undoubtedly a terrifying place to be for young Parfitt and his comrades. They arrived there at around 7.30am, and were soon after 'greeted' by storming German troops, firing and blasting at them, while having to avoid mines and other traps that had been left in wait. A friend of Parfitt's in the regiment, John Lincoln, later wrote a book about their battalion called *Thank God and the Infantry*, in which he quoted a comrade of theirs, Lieutenant Eric Woodhouse, describing their arrival in France.

Woodhouse said:

> *After the D-Day landing on Sword beach, memories of details are rather vague, but the overall impression was a hell of a lot of noise, explosions, smoke, clutter of bodies and our main thoughts centred on objectives to be achieved on shore.*

The significance of Sword beach in the context of the whole of the operation was its closeness to the city of Caen. Caen was about nine miles to the south of the beach and a vital city to re-take as soon as possible because of the many roads and railway tracks that went through it. It was an important centre for Germany's transport and communication links (also for the Allies).

As mentioned above, the boys and men in Parfitt's battalion were far from alone along the five-mile length of Sword beach. On D-Day, a staggering 29,000 Allied troops landed on the sand, pebbles and even in the sea – by parachute, or on one of the hundreds of navy vessels deployed to deliver them. Thousands of

regular troops took the enemy to task in tanks, with guns and by dropping bombs. The 'regulars' were supported by Commandos – super-tough troops specially trained to serve in very challenging and often secret raids, of which there were many on D-Day, and the days that followed.

The Germans lost many more men in the fighting at Sword beach on 6 June than the Allies, but, sadly, more than 600 Allies lost their lives too. These were exhausted men, some of whom never got beyond the sand dunes to begin their onward journey east and south. Parfitt, however, did make his get-away from Sword, several hours later, on foot, towards Caen – and he moved on for a week or so, with his comrades via other towns that also needed to be retaken, such as Merville and Ouistreham, and over many of the bridges that were targets for the taking, too. At all times, the men had to be alert to the dangers of the encroaching or hidden enemy. Every day during the campaign to liberate France, the Allies made advances, but those advances in turn strengthened German resolve not to lose the battle without very fierce and determined defence.

Captain Parfitt did not make it to Caen. He almost did, but was inflicted with terrible wounds that resulted in him being taken to the mortuary tent (albeit incorrectly, because he was not dead!) during an offensive in an area called Lébisy Wood, just to the north of their target city of Caen. Perhaps it was a blessing he didn't make it to Caen – the Allies had a far tougher battle recapturing it than they anticipated. They finally reclaimed the city on 19 July, but it took six weeks rather than their hoped-for single day. To win back Caen, 6,000 bombs were dropped, which destroyed 80 per cent of the city; and 30,000 Allied troops lost their lives. What a horrible, devastating business war is, even when victory can be claimed.

Returning to our hero of the chapter, Captain Parfitt, who battled bravely with his comrades in the 1st until he suddenly, but not quite, met his match. He is quoted in John Lincoln's book, about the time he was attacked, saying:

After severe wounds and a brave rescue by Sergeant Savage, my evacuation from Lébisy Wood began. Firstly, to the Battalion First Aid point, then onwards strapped to the roof of a jeep. My companion was a young German lieutenant (in civilian life a music student from Heidelberg) who had lost both feet through stepping on a mine.

Finally, the Base Field Hospital near an airfield was reached. By this time, I was drifting into unconsciousness – up to this point I had remained just awake, despite a massive loss of blood and pain-killing injections.

At the Field Hospital, I remember very little of what was happening. However, at dawn the next morning I recollect being surrounded by what seemed to be 'white haze'; and, trying to twitch the stiff fingers of my left hand, alerted the attention of a ~~Queen~~ Alexandra Nursing Sister, going off duty from the night shift.

She hastened over to my stretcher and moistened my lips with some grapes she was carrying, and I was able to greet her.

Soon afterwards two shocked medical orderlies moved me into intensive care. My fellow wounded seemed surprised and shocked, then I was told I had been in the mortuary! After further specialist attention I was given a place on a plane, with an attendant nurse and an oxygen tube, to be flown back to the UK for urgent surgery.

Some are born lucky!

The survival of the horses

I was given Cecil Parfitt's Second World War story by his son Rob, who lives in Suffolk. I spent a fascinating day with him reading letters, hearing anecdotes and looking at lots of documents and photographs. Rob talked to me about some of what he remembers about his father, and of what his father was most thankful for during his long life. Cecil died in 1998, aged 81.

'My father was a gentleman', said Rob, 'and he would always seek reconciliation in times of conflict; for example, even though he was so hurt by them, he wouldn't hear a bad word said about the Germans. He always said we had to live alongside them. And he loved Norfolk, too; I think he felt he was lucky to live in this part of the country for almost all of his life.'

It isn't surprising, therefore, that when he signed up to be part of the war effort he did so with The Royal Norfolk's, his local regiment.

The Royal Norfolk's (now part of the 1st East Anglian Regiment, since joining with the Suffolk regiment in 1959) have a long and colourful history, dating back to 1685, when King James II was on the throne. The regiment suffered a terrible defeat during the War of the Spanish Succession (1701–14) when the entire unit was captured and taken to France as prisoners of war. However, a prisoner exchange followed, and the regiment recovered. In 1751, it was renamed the 9th Regiment of Foot – so-called because it was an infantry regiment, and its name describes how the troops performed their service. During the intervening centuries, its infantrymen have been part of conflicts all over the world, including in many of the most well-known battles such as the American War of Independence (1775–83), the Napoleonic Wars (1803–15), the Crimean War (1854–56), the Burma Campaign in 1888, the Boer War (1899–1902) and they served during the First World War on the Western Front, and in Mesopotamia (modern-day Iraq), in the Middle East. Five of its servicemen were awarded the Victoria Cross for courage during the Second World War – more than any other regiment.

One of the documents Rob shared with me was

a letter sent to him by a war-time comrade, shortly after his father died, in which he described their battalion, the 1st; and wrote of how Captain Parfitt was viewed by their comrades. He wrote:

The 1st Battalion, the Royal Norfolk Regiment, was a regular service battalion. We had, at the time your dad joined, approximately 60 per cent regular soldiers and 40 per cent were soldiers either called-up or young and volunteered. There was every kind of man you could think of; some were utter snobs, and some were foul-mouthed and terrible bullies. Many of our battalion thought, at first, when we landed on D-Day and up to the time your dad was terribly wounded, that he was either very stupid or completely mad. We soon realised he wasn't stupid or mad, he was very brave and had no fear. I think when your dad was hit by pieces of the shell, it is possible he was as near to death as any human could be, but he was so brave.

It is hard for many of us to understand this kind of courage and bravery. I was terrified all the time. The only thing that kept me from showing my fear was the fear of others knowing I was frightened.

I will always remember your dad and was proud to have known him, and I know I am a better man for having known him.

Finally, Rob spoke to me about his father's love of animals, particularly dogs and horses. He showed me photographs of some of his father's most loved pets over the years, including Heidi, a Staffordshire bull terrier, and Fran and Laila, his spaniels. Even in the toughest of conditions during his time in France in the war, shortly after his arrival, Cecil extended his care to two wounded horses, which had probably been left to die. Quoted in John Lincoln's book, he said:

The Victoria Cross medal is the United Kingdom's highest award for military bravery and devotion to duty.

Within a day or two of my arrival in Normandy, I noticed a fine pair of hunters wandering free near a demolished barn. I was astonished at their survival given how much shrapnel was embedded in their hides. A little later, I bumped into George Seaman, another horse lover, and expressed my deep concern at

ANIMALS IN WORLD WAR TWO

* German Shepherds, Labradors and Dobermans served as watch dogs in charge of protecting supplies. They were also trained to find soldiers and civilians trapped under debris and could even be taught to sniff out hidden mines!

* Cats were also crucial to the protection of supplies. While dogs would alert soldiers to human thieves, cats were invaluable when it came to keeping mice and rats out of the store cupboards!

* Around 250,000 carrier pigeons were used by Britain during the war, carrying vital messages across enemy lines and in some cases, having small cameras strapped to their chests in order to take images from the skies.

* As well as fulfilling specific duties, thousands of animals provided companionship to soldiers across the globe that proved just as important as any other role. Soldiers often credited their animal friends as being crucial to their mental wellbeing during the darkest of times.

* During both the First and Second World Wars, pack animals such as horses and donkeys would carry heavy guns and ammunition, as well as food and medical supplies. They were especially useful on uneven landscapes in remote areas.

the deterioration of the animals' wounds. To cut a long story short, we decided to have a go at removing the shrapnel; at least that near the surface.

At dusk, George returned with a dagger, with a sharp point and twin edge. It was quite a game catching and haltering the animals, the risk from their frantic kicks being almost more lethal than the occasional mortar shell falling uncomfortably close. However, once we had removed some of the metal the first horse stood still, waiting for us to carry on, it seemed.

More remarkable still to find the other animal calmly standing, waiting for his turn…

It is rare when writing about the devastation of war to think about animals and the destruction to nature it causes, too. Quite naturally, and unsurprisingly, we focus on the losses to humankind; but the devastation of war is much more far-reaching than the deaths of people. When bombs were dropped, they fell on animals too, and trees, fields and hedgerows that take years to re-plant and re-grow. Aeroplanes unintentionally slaughtered birds and insects in the sky; and in the oceans, submarines, ships and torpedoes caused terrible interruption to the eco-system, killing fish, whales and thousands of other sea creatures in their wake.

I am grateful to Cecil for his love of animals, and nature, because of him I have been able to write about the impact of war on our environment. We human beings will have a wonderful world if we look after it – but it will certainly not be wonderful if we don't.

Carrier pigeons and their British Army owners at the end of the war in 1945.

CHAPTER SIX

MADY GERRARD

AUNT GISI'S LEGACY AND THE HOLOCAUST

With mountain views, lakeside shoreline, cobbled streets and a splendid Baroque palace, Keszthely (pronounced Kezthlee) is a congenial market town in the west of Hungary, in Eastern Europe – I hope to visit one day. Mady Gerrard, who has sadly since passed away, told me all about it. Keszthely was the place of her childhood home, where she was happily brought up by her Uncle Joseph and Aunt Gisella, whom she loved very dearly. Her mother died when she was only seven, and her father worked away so much that he needed someone else to take care of his daughter.

The mountains that overlook the town form part of the Bakony mountain range. Mady recalled how scenic she had found the 'Bakonies', not least of all because they are heavily forested and she loved trees and flowers. Keszthely is also home to a large lake, called Lake Balaton; just under 50 miles (80 kilometres) from east to west, it is the largest freshwater lake in central Europe. Sometimes in the winter, Mady said, its surface froze enough to skate on it, and very often in the summer it was warm enough to swim in. There was also a palace, called the Festetics Palace, which dates back to 1745. It is now a museum with a library, art gallery and gardens. With a population of 20,000, Keszthely is big enough to have everything one might need (including greengrocers, bakeries, butchers, and playgrounds), but is also small enough to feel safe and comfortable.

Growing up in an environment bursting with natural beauty was a blessing, Mady recalled during our conversation. She also spoke very kindly of her uncle and aunt – particularly her aunt, who she affectionately referred to as Aunt Gisi. 'I learnt so much from my little great aunt', she said. 'She taught me everything. She was so good to me; my mother wouldn't have been any better.'

These lifelong lessons, for which Mady was always grateful, included being taught how to sew. Not only basic stitching, but sophisticated skills of proper dressmaking. She told me her Aunt Gisi taught her how to design and create clothes with nothing but a needle and a swathe of material, as well as how to knit and how to crochet. The love of dressmaking that her 'dear Aunt Gisi' instilled upon Mady never left her, and later in her life she set up a very successful fashion business of her own, designing and sewing to her heart's content.

These skills of creativity proved to be useful during the Second World War for Mady. I will tell you why…

March 1944

Mady Gerrard was ten years old when the Second World War began in September 1939. For a while, she – a Jew, as were her uncle and aunt and most of the population of Keszthely – were largely unaffected by what was happening in the world around them. In the early years of the war, Hungary supported Germany in its battle against Russia. This was a good thing for the people of Hungary – for a while they were safe and life, for them, continued much as normal. However, what most of the Hungarian population did not know was that their Prime Minister, Miklós Kállay, was also in talks with the British Prime Minister Winston Churchill and the Americans (under President Roosevelt). Prime Minister Kállay suggested to Britain and the USA that if Allied troops were able to come to Hungary, he would consider switching his allegiance to the Allies.

When Germany, under Adolf Hitler, found out in September 1943 that Hungary was considering a 'betrayal', it was furious, and by March 1944, Germany gave up hope of Hungarian support. Many of the people in this small, land-locked Eastern European country were made to pay the price of their leader's decision.

The beating heart of Mady's precious home town, in common with many other similarly sized towns in Hungary and its capital, Budapest, almost stopped as the Germans took over the country and the Jewish people – most people in

FACT FILE

ADOLF HITLER

* He was born on 20 April 1889 and died on 30 April 1945.

* He ruled Germany as head of the Nazi Party from 1933 to 1945 and called himself Führer ('Leader').

* He believed that Germans were born to rule over other people, and wished to remove all Jewish people from society.

* He would not allow anyone to disagree with him, and severely punished or killed anyone that tried.

* His hatred eventually led to more than six million Jewish people dying in the Holocaust.

Hungary were Jews – were suddenly denied their freedom, but far worse, thousands did not live to see the end of the war.

Mady, then just 14 years old, was one of those whose life was completely changed by what happened in her country in March 1944. The tragedy that unfolded was called the Holocaust – it resulted in the early deaths at concentration camps of some six million Jews, not only from Hungary but many other countries including Poland, Russia and Romania. Thousands of others were killed too, simply because they were disabled.

Completely undeserving of punishment, once in the camps people were made to work very hard and had very little to eat. Also, many died after being ordered into rooms called gas chambers, where their lives ended because the gas they breathed in was poisonous. Mady's uncle and aunt were two of the millions of people who died in one of these chambers. Mady lost her best friend, too, a little girl called Lilly. These bereavements were very sad for Mady – she was so young to have to cope with such loss, and every day she was there, she feared for her own life.

Mady spent time in two camps (she was moved from one to another after six months) for more than a year. She became very thin because she rarely had enough to eat; but there were rare moments of brightness in the darkness of the Holocaust. She told me about one of the slightly 'brighter moments', which, unsurprisingly for Mady, involved creating something. Of course, she didn't have any lovely threads to stitch with, or silky fabrics to delight in, but at least she had an opportunity to put her creative skills to the test. In doing so, she was rewarded with some much-

needed extra bread and, she told me, also giving some joy to some of the female guards at the camp who were 'quite simply', Mady said, 'utterly miserable about what they were being forced to do'.

Wispy-thin, electrical wire…

It was while Mady was being held at a camp called Bergen-Belsen in northern Germany, towards the end of the war that she, and some of the other young girls were given some work to sort out thin electrical wires. She told me:

Our job was to pull out the wire from the coloured outside cover, and the covers were made of small beads. The beads were perfect for necklaces, so we started to make some and gave them to the German ladies in charge of us, who were really pleased with them. They gave us some extra bread and margarine, in exchange for the little necklaces. After all, they didn't have much either, so it worked for everyone.

So it was, because of these delicate little necklaces that she taught her friends how to make, that she was able to share a little bit of joy with those who made them, and with those who received them.

The outside world, again!

Mady, by now 15 years old, was freed from Bergen-Belsen at the end of the war in April 1945. She, and some others, were found by members of British special forces who were undertaking reconnaissance (military observation) in northern Germany – which meant they were looking for people, like Mady, who needed help or rescue.

The British soldiers who found her looked after her wonderfully, and the war had ended by then, so, suddenly she had no need to worry for her own safety anymore. The soldiers arranged for her to go to Sweden to be cared for by members of the Swedish Red Cross at a special centre for orphans of war.

What a contrast for her to the weeks and months before; once again (like Keszthely), she saw mountains and water, she had a comfortable bed, plenty of food, but most of all she was loved and safe. Of this time, she said, 'My journey to Sweden was an unreal dream after the nightmare I had experienced. I saw the Northern Lights and was fed and cared for so diligently by the staff that in less than two months I had doubled in weight, going from 25kg to 60kg. I was chubby! But better to be chubby and alive, than skinny and dead!'

Back to Keszthely

When she returned to Keszthely, she was delighted to see the 'Bakonies' were still lovingly and protectively looking over the town; the water of Lake Balaton was as clean and fresh as it ever was; the Festetics Palace had remained intact; and the cobbles on the small streets could still be felt underfoot. However, it was a very different town to the one she left in March 1944. Russia, led

by its leader Joseph Stalin, was now running Hungary; and had positioned guards and tanks on the streets, noisily repressing the spirits of those who had remained and – like Mady – returned. Mady recalled how shocked she was by how poor the people who were left behind had become and she said that even though the palace was not bombed, it too, was a place of sadness:

So much in the palace was removed as souvenirs, or more likely firewood. If the war-stricken people were so poor and so desperate for wood during that really difficult time, who can blame them for taking what they needed? So much that was good and worthwhile in Keszthely was ruined – even the old wood-block floors that had been made years before were destroyed…

So much of Eastern Europe looked very sad after the war ended. The people were downtrodden, they were badly dressed and very poor; buildings had been destroyed and food was far from plentiful.

Ten years later

Mady lived in Keszthely for ten years after the war ended, during which time she slowly began to build up her fashion business, which eventually took her to England and America; and finally, Wales. During this time, Mady was able to see the small green shoots of recovery in her town; families appearing and growing, people once again shopping in the town, swimming in the lake,

HUNGARY AND ITS JEWISH POPULATION

* Even before the full Nazi occupation of Hungary, the country already had a strong history of antisemitism (prejudice and hostility against Jewish people).

* When Hungary joined the war in 1941, approximately 100,000 Jewish men were forced to participate in the labour service, and were subjected to extreme violence and often not allowed access to clothes, food and medical care.

* As time went on, regulations forced Jewish people to hand over their cars, telephones, radios and bicycles, as well as other property.

* In March 1944, when Germany invaded Hungary, there were between 760,000 and 780,000 Jews living in the country – the largest Jewish population still alive in Europe.

* Shortly after the invasion, all Jews over the age of six were forced to wear a Star of David (a common Jewish symbol) as a method of identification.

* Within the next year alone, Germans and its Hungarian collaborators would murder approximately 500,000 Jews.

In Hungary's capital city, Budapest, there is a memorial to all who lost their lives called Shoes on the Danube Bank.

playing in the playground, walking in the mountains – and eating langos, a speciality of Hungary that is a warm potato bun topped with cheese, cream and sometimes bacon.

The shadow of the Holocaust will never go away; it will always be there. It is important that we know of such happenings and thank people like Mady who lived through it and have been brave enough to tell their story. Only by knowing of the Holocaust can we begin to understand it, a little bit; and, most importantly, understand that it must never – ever – happen again.

John Randall, who has now died, was one of the young men who rescued Mady, more than 75 years ago now. He said, 'In spite of what the survivors lived through, they have a history of extraordinary bravery, a determination to survive and the indomitable spirit to never give up hope. This must be an inspiration to all of us.'

CHAPTER SEVEN

BILL CARTER

THE RAF AND THE MIDDLE EAST

Petrol Tin Island

Petrol Tin Island is the nickname of a landmass that was little more than a giant sand dune in the middle of the Middle East where Bill Carter, a senior RAF engineer, spent almost a year, during the Second World War.

The island's real name is Masirah, but it was called Petrol Tin Island because when Bill, and his fellow squadron members, arrived there early in 1943, they found it littered with empty four-gallon petrol tins, which they filled with sand, piled up and draped tarpaulin over, creating more than adequate 'homes' for themselves. It was a satisfying start to what otherwise might have been an uncomfortable year of sleeping under the stars among creatures previously unknown, and temperatures fluctuating so much it was as though the air couldn't make up its mind what it wanted to be.

Most of the empty tins had been dumped by crewmen from the nearby Kingdom of Oman. They had been transporting petrol for Allied crews who were flying Wellington bombers on patrol duties in the Persian Gulf, the Arabian Sea, and parts of the nearby Indian Ocean. These sea channels were important Allied supply routes, which needed protection from enemy submarines; the danger of which, in this area, and in the Atlantic, could not be underestimated.

Bill Carter, and his comrades in 5153 Squadron, were sent to the uninhabited island of Masirah to build an aerodrome, needed for the visiting aircrews. It was hot, hard work and everything had to be brought to them, even water had to be delivered. Their deliveries, including food and building supplies, mostly arrived on 100-ton barges from Oman, Saudi Arabia and Pakistan. Together with labourers and engineers from many other Allied countries, an organised system of drilling wells and levelling sand began. Firstly, Bill told me, they built a sanitation block, then roads and a runway followed. During the day their work was carried out under the fierce heat of the sun, and at night paraffin flares lit up the darkness.

Turtles

I had to find out from Bill, too, how on earth they sustained themselves, fearing they might have been hungry a lot of the time. He told me the food was, mostly, 'hard tack' (meaning pretty horrible); except when they were 'spoilt rotten' by officials from Oman who would sometimes stay on the island. When they did so, they would bring plentiful supplies of delicious local food, including lots of meat and fish, which they were delighted to share. The trouble was, Bill told me, 'The first time we dined like this we all ate far too much – because it is an Omani custom to give a diner more food when their plate is empty – unless you indicate you are full by turning over your cup. But we didn't know this custom, so they kept giving us more and more!'

Now to the turtles, for whom, prior to the arrival of 5153 and the other men, Masirah had, I expect, been an idyllic home.

There were hundreds of them; they were everywhere. It was obvious that from the moment of our arrival the turtles, and their eggs, were going to be a key part of our diet. The turtles would come out of the water up to the beach, venture on to the land for about 100 yards and lay their eggs in clusters of around 50 in the sandhills. Each egg was around the size of a table tennis ball, but with soft shells that had to be gently pulled open to get to the food inside. Turtle eggs can't really be compared to a cooked chicken egg because the white will always refuse to set – no matter how long it is cooked, it remains viscous and runny – unpalatable, unless you were terribly hungry.

(Not my idea of an ideal lunch!)

Мальчик, который является прекрасным кусок трубы

Don't panic! Unless you are either Russian, or studying the language, the above words won't mean anything to you. Translated into English, it means 'Boy that is a fine piece of pipe'! Why am I telling you this? Because it is part of Bill Carter's story – Bill told me how much he enjoyed the company of many of the men from other countries he came to know during his year in Masirah Island, Oman, highlighting lively conversations he had especially with Russians and Czechoslovakians. Learning each other's languages helped them in their work, and it passed the time, too. In fact, from the way that Bill described his Masirah memories, there was rarely a dull moment.

No one could hide

During the war no one, wherever they were, whatever they were doing, or why they were doing it, could escape the fury being played out in the world, and the uncertainty that it unleashed. For Bill, the sadness of his war was that he was a long way from home, tasked with working on an island that would have rarely been peaceful because of the constant drone of enormous four-engine bombers flying overhead, reminding him of the perils not far away, and of the dangers he knew so many of his friends and family were facing daily. However, Bill had a 'secret weapon', a way of coping that gave him inner strength, that enabled him to cheer and strengthen his comrades. His secret weapon was music.

Bill's musical war

A trained pianist, Bill told me it was rare not to have a tune playing in his head, and his Second World War years were no exception. Often, he said, he'd gather the lads around after a long day's work on the aerodrome in Masirah and they'd end the day blasting out a rousing tune, sometimes hymns to remind them of home, other times sea shanties or popular songs of the day, such as 'I'll be Seeing You' and 'The White Cliffs of Dover'.

Bill told me, too, of his one night of 'actually being a proper pop star'. Towards the end of the war, he was stationed at a transit camp in Benghazi in Libya, looking after Italian prisoners-of-war. The then very famous American baritone Nelson Eddy visited, as part of a tour he was undertaking for Allied troops in the area. Fortunately for Bill, Eddy's right-hand man who played the piano for him was unwell that evening and Bill was asked to stand in. He told me he kept the 'stars in his eyes' forever after that!

Bill's next story tells us a more sombre memory, but one that still illustrates the comfort that music can bring. It takes us back to before Bill's arrival in the Middle East; during his journey to this part of the world, previously completely unknown to him.

Bill began his wartime journey in May 1942, setting sail on board the ship *Dominion Monarch*, from the Firth of Clyde in Scotland. His was one of a large convoy of vessels travelling eastwards. The whole convoy travelled far into the Atlantic Ocean before heading south, avoiding enemy submarines (U-boats) as much as possible.

However, this was possibly the time during the war that Bill was most exposed to danger – as were all the men on board all the ships. They knew at any point a sub could be lurking. Sadly, the convoy did not escape attack, no less than four ships went down in sight of Bill and his friends on their boat, and they could do nothing, except despair and hope they would not be next.

Not long after the tragedy of the losses, Bill told me they arrived at Cape Town harbour – where the *Dominion Monarch*

The Dominion Monarch.

stopped to refuel, and its crew were able to disembark and stretch their legs. However, what Bill remembers most about this stop, and something he told me was 'simply wonderful', was hearing a lady in the harbour singing to them as loudly as she could, as the ship pulled in. She was singing Arthur Benson's 'Land of Hope and Glory', set to music by Edward Elgar. Bill said, 'To see her, and listen to her contralto tones was a delight, and the timing could not have been better. It was truly comforting for all of us to be reminded of England like that.'

Below are the words – your parents and teachers will know the tune – have a lovely sing-along. I am sure Bill Carter would want you to.

LAND OF HOPE AND GLORY

CHAPTER EIGHT

RAY EDWARDS

A CHILD'S WAR IN THE SUFFOLK COUNTRYSIDE

Ray was a 'bor' of only six years on the day the Second World War was announced in September 1939, and by the time it ended he had just passed his twelfth birthday. These are 'formative years'; meaning this is the time of life where we learn more quickly than at any other time, so it is perhaps not surprising that he remembers so much about his Second World War childhood. As this is written, Ray is 88 years old and living in the same part of rural Suffolk as he lived as a child and has resided in for almost all his life. (Hence the use of the word bor, which is the local dialect for the word boy.) Ray is justifiably proud of his Suffolk origins and speaks in the local dialect with contentment that this part of the country – close to the market towns of Beccles and Halesworth – has always been his home.

I have, happily, come to know Ray Edwards well since first meeting him more than seven years ago (as this is written). He has told me much about his life; including telling me of his family, especially his wife Joan, to whom he was married for 59 years until she died in 2018, and about his children, twins Gillian and Paul, and youngest daughter, Andrea. During his working years, he served for a while in the RAF as an aircraft engineer between 1951 and 1954 based at Tern Hill in Shropshire, and Spalding Moor in Yorkshire. However, most of his career was in Suffolk, working on farms and caring for properties for Suffolk County Council education committee, ending his work with the authority as a manager.

This chapter and introduction to Ray, would be incomplete without a mention of his garden; it is here that I have learnt most about his war-time childhood, which he recalled with a sharpness of memory that is quite remarkable given almost eight decades have passed in between. His garden has an abundance of fruit trees, plum, pear and apple; but what perhaps makes it even more special is the range of geraniums, snowdrops and cyclamen Ray has cultivated over the years. There is something very special about listening to someone reminisce about years past in a garden. His garden contains many shrubs and plants planted relatively recently, but also there are trees old enough to have weathered the Second World War, too. I write especially of an old Scots pine that is probably more than 150 years old that stands in the corner of his garden as proudly today as it would have done during the Second World War and the First World War. If only trees could talk…

Now – to the war

As mentioned earlier, Ray was only six when the war started. He had two older brothers – Ronnie and George, and a younger sister, Ann. Ronnie, the eldest and about seven years older than Ray, was accepted into the RAF in 1943 – much to the surprise, and worry, of his parents. Ray is proud of Ronnie to this day; you will find out more about his story later in this chapter.

The Edwards family lived in a large farmhouse in the tiny Suffolk village of Uggeshall; they were one of three families sharing the house, which was neatly divided into three cottage-style dwellings, each one having two rooms upstairs and two down. Ray said for the first few years of his life he would bathe in a tin bath (the water was heated in a 'copper' beneath it) in the corner of the kitchen, but eventually the bath and copper were moved into a tin shed in the garden to make more living space in the house. This, Ray said: 'was good because it was such a squash in the house, but it was grim in the winter to get out of a hot bath and run through the freezing night air to the back door, only having a candle in a jar to light the way in the dark'.

He also said he had had the freedom of the fields and woods as soon as he could walk, and that he would wander around alone, never bored, because there was so much to see and explore. He remembered in the spring, as he grew up, picking huge bunches of primroses for his mother, helping to decorate the local church.

Fortunately for Ray, he didn't lose this freedom with the onset of war. He continued to roam the countryside that surrounded him, possibly in a slightly less carefree way. His parents urged vigilance, but there was little they could practically do when he was out of sight. I expect they didn't know about many of the things he got up to, such as the day he got off his school bus and hid under a small road bridge that was being approached by a convoy of large tanks. He realised afterwards how close the bridge came to collapsing under the weight of the tanks and how foolish it was to hide under it!

The village of Uggeshall had been designated by the War Office as a battle training ground, therefore exposing the Edwards family (and their neighbours) to greater dangers than they might otherwise have been subjected to. Ray said:

At the beginning of the war, we were given notice to move because there was a thought it would be too risky for us to stay. But after a while we were told we could stay after all and my father was told that if the Germans landed locally, he was to help round up the livestock and herd them behind our lines of defence, so they were available to milk and to be slaughtered as meat for our troops.

Ray continued to talk of the war as an exciting, if fearful, time for a young boy. He recalled noticing, even though he was very young, how tense and worried his parents were; saying that their fears were, in part, exacerbated by the news of what was happening around the rest of the country and the world, which came to them on the radio. His father was not conscripted into one of the forces because he was a farmworker / cowman, which was a reserved occupation, and one very important for providing people with food. As we saw in Peter Blackburn's chapter, other reserved occupations included teachers, plumbers, vicars and doctors.

Of his parents, he said:

They never had idle hands! During the war, my father would get up at 4.30am, every day, to hand-milk the cows. He came in for breakfast, but didn't have a break until midday, when he would do a bit of gardening. His day usually finished at about 5pm but there would be overtime, when he would chop sugar beet, cart hay, or do some harvesting, if it was the season.

He was also a member of the nightly fire-watch team working a rota of nights on and off duty. It was also during this time he had a terrible embarrassment. He had a white coat to wear when he was doing his 'cowman work' _ and my mother washed it almost every day to keep it as clean as possible. One day, after hunting around in the darkness of the cottage in the early hours of the morning after doing a fireman shift, he picked up my mother's nightie instead of his cowman coat and had to milk the cows wearing the frilly nightie!

I remember my mother, as well as looking after us, doing lots of knitting. She had a machine that would make socks. This was done by turning a handle and out would come scores of khaki and aircraft-blue socks. Many times I was reluctantly roped in to 'turn', or hold out my hands while she wound the wool from hank to ball. Mother also helped served tea and snacks to the soldiers at the local canteen, sometimes having to cycle quite a long way in the dark.

Looking back, my parents had a very heavy workload. We children did help too – we quite happily completed our chores for our sixpence a week pocket money. My brothers chopped sticks and cleaned the privy; I cleaned shoes or ran errands, for the neighbours too.

The Second World War was, to some extent, a war of two halves for the people of East Anglia (where Suffolk is based) because the American Eighth Army arrived in the summer of 1942. This was a huge 'army' of thousands of American air force personnel located in more than 100 airfields in this area alone. They were, in general, very friendly and integrated well with the local people – fondly remembered by many for their bountiful supplies of such things as chewing gum, peanut butter and Coca Cola, which they often shared.

However, what Ray remembers most about the Americans is the aircraft they flew. They had huge fleets of B-17 Flying Fortresses and B-24 Liberators, with crews of 10 and 11 in each. These planes were enormous; both with wingspans of more than 100 feet, and around 65 feet long. They were Allied planes, but Ray said he still felt afraid when, often, more than one would fly above him roaring, almost unbearably deafening, and threatening.

He said:

The skies over Uggeshall throbbed with the noise of enormous aircraft during the latter years of the war; British bombers by night, American by day. The Americans would gather in numbers of many hundreds from the airfields of East Anglia to form a huge Armada of aircraft directly overhead, before flying away on their operation. 'Shepherd planes' would fly in the front, firing flares in various colour formations, showing the other aircraft where to go. These 'shepherds' would return to base once the others were in position.

On their return from a raid some of the aircraft would be in a sorry state, with engines on fire, huge holes in the wings and wheels hanging loose. Often airmen could be seen throwing out everything movable just to stay in the air. I remember being very frightened and always hoping and praying they would return to the ground safely.

His saddest wartime memory relates to these aircraft. He said:

I remember, when we were at school one day, a huge flight of American bombers flew overhead. It was very noisy and there was an awful crashing, crunching sound — two had collided and fell to the ground. We could see and smell the smoke. Not long after, the bombs they were carrying exploded too… there was debris all over the place. Thirty-seven people died that day – and lots of the people who went to help them got burnt too. What a terrible memory.

Ray Edwards' Second World War 'trophy' moment is also a schoolboy memory; thankfully one with a happy ending! So far, I have painted a picture of Ray – I think – as a rather angelic child; a lover of the countryside, and a willing errand-runner. However, on this occasion he was quite naughty. But as you will read, Ray (so called because his mother said he was a 'ray of sunshine' when he was born) got away with this gung-ho act of dare and do. He said:

I think it was late 1942 – Ronnie came home with an unexploded incendiary bomb that he had found in a sugar-beet field. After he made it safe by taking it to pieces and burning the contents (he knew what he was doing because he was in the Home Guard, and had been taught how to detonate an explosive), he gave it to me. I thought this was so amazing that I, without telling anyone, decided to take it to school. Although I knew, of course, it was strictly forbidden to do that sort of thing, how couldn't I? The other boys only had bits of shrapnel and shell cases – I had a real bomb! I remember showing the boys and the teacher wanting to find out why I had suddenly become centre of attention (I wasn't usually). She sent for the police, and I had a lot of explaining to do – and was left in no doubt what would happen if I ever brought a bomb into school again.

However, to my amazement they let me have it back to take home, thank goodness, because Ronnie would have been furious to lose it. Years later, my father buried it, with all the shell cases we had collected. But at least I'd had my fun.

Brother Ronnie

I came to know Ray because he kindly contacted me after reading one of my earlier Second World War books. Initially, Ray just wanted to tell me about Ronnie, not about himself, but I am glad, of course, I have come to hear his own story. However, as I mentioned earlier, Ray is very proud of Ronnie (who died in 1995), so we need to remember his wartime experience in the RAF, too.

Ray told me that when Ronnie decided he want to sign up to serve in the RAF there was: 'no stopping him. After a day's hoeing sugar-beet, he suddenly laid his coat over the handlebars of his bicycle and cycled off to Ipswich, 30 miles away, still wearing his working clothes, to sign up, not even telling mother. He wasn't accepted then but six months later, in September 1943, they took him on and he survived 30 operations as a rear gunner on Lancasters.'

As we first heard in Ivor Foster's chapter, the four-engine Lancaster bomber aircraft, with a wingspan of more than 100 feet and around 70 feet long, was the largest of the RAF's bombers flown during the war. It is described in more detail in John Ottewell's chapter in this book.

Being a rear-gunner in a Lancaster was one of the most precarious of all roles undertaken in all the armed forces during the war. Despite the size of the aircraft and the speed it was able to achieve, rear-gunners were very vulnerable. Ronnie was one of its seven crew members; seated at the back of the plane, his job was to look out for enemy action – and shoot when necessary. Most of the operations Ronnie took part in were over heavily defended Germany, when the aircraft would have been shot at from all directions, including bullets coming from below. However, Ray said he remembered Ronnie telling him how difficult it was to see – and sometimes he would 'confuse even a speck of dirt for an enemy fighter' – not least of all because the goggles they had to wear often clouded their vision.

Ronnie would have known, as did all rear gunners, that he was even more exposed to the likelihood of being killed while in the sky than other members of the crew because the Luftwaffe (the German Air Force) pilots, as a rule, chose to attack aircraft first at the rear. More than 20,000 of Britain's Bomber Command's rear gunners did not survive the war – representing a greater loss rate than any other position. Hence the delight and relief of Ray, and his parents, when Ronnie returned in May 1945.

Ronnie's most dangerous wartime moment was during D-Day, in June 1944, when the Allies liberated France after four years of occupation. Ray told me:

Two of Ronnie's Lancaster engines were blown out and 80 holes were made in the fuselage, with at least one large enough to put a fist through. Ronnie told me he was being repeatedly shot at and some shrapnel got into his turret and circled around. He said his pilot saved the day for them, keeping calm in the storm of blasts and bullets, flying the aircraft as though it was a boat on a choppy ocean, tipping it so it wasn't level even for a moment. Ronnie called this 'yawing' and 'cork-screwing' — he said he is sure it saved his life.

Finally...

As our conversation drew to a close, it suddenly felt very peaceful in Ray's garden. I looked up at the sky; a calm, pale blue canopy with white and grey clouds gathering, but no aircraft, the sounds of bombers years ago replaced with birdsong and the odd rumble of a car driving past. However, Ray suddenly broke the tranquility, remembering to tell me about a Nissen hut that is still hidden somewhere in the undergrowth in Uggeshall, that had served during the war as an underground bunker for the Secret Home Guard where (often deadly) enemy attacks would have been planned. 'The hut is still there,' Ray said. 'The Second World War will always be with us, and we must remember those who gave us our freedom today.'

CHAPTER NINE

PAT RORKE

BLETCHLEY AND BEYOND – DECODING AND BURMA

AJDKSIRUXBLHWTMCQGZNPYFVOE

Why would I start this chapter, Pat Rorke's story, like that? I'll tell you why – because the letters of the alphabet, presented in such a sequence, are an example of a very important code called Enigma; the decoding of which Pat Rorke, now 97 years old, told me all about.

Pat was 18 years old in 1942 when she first discovered that thousands of coded messages were zipping around the world – written by the enemy as well as the Allies – and containing vital information about planned operations, targets of attack, instructions from high command; and so much more. Successfully coded messages were ones that could only be encrypted by those for whom they were intended; but successful coding in itself would not have been enough to win the war – it was essential, too, that the coded messages of the enemy could be intercepted, and decoded.

After years of practice (including before the war officially began in September 1939), and using a variety of complex machines (some of which were like typewriters and others were like mechanical wheels with rotor-blades), an extraordinarily clever team of code-breakers, who worked undercover from a large country house called Bletchley Park in Buckinghamshire, became increasingly successful at translating enemy code, and writing their own, that – for the most part – sufficiently out-witted the enemy.

Burma – Pat Rorke's beloved homeland

When the war broke out in September 1939, Pat was 18 years old, and living in a country called Burma (now Myanmar), next to India, with her family, where she had grown up.

Burma, however, became too dangerous for them to stay after bombing began in December 1941, and they were forced to leave, travelling to India for safety. After her arrival there, she found work in an intelligence-receiving office in New Delhi, which took in Enigma-coded messages to be used by those in High Command – to give as much information as they could to army generals and navy commanders about the whereabouts of the enemy. Pat, however, was very sad about her departure from her

homeland, recalling some touching memories: 'I remember exotic bottle-birds that hung their woven nests in the Palmyra palms growing in the garden, and kites that circled above the trees.' She said, too, that she and her elder sister Eileen would sit together, 'with our backs against the wooden wall of the house, just talking'.

'Life was full of wonder', she told me. She recalled having 'so much to think about and dream about'.

However, while the natural world was a delight and comfort to her as she grew up, Burma was not an especially peaceful country, and she first came to realise how unkind people could be to each other in the 1930s, when Rangoon – then the Burmese capital (it is now Naypyitdaw) – was engulfed in riots, between the Burmese people and troops from British-controlled India, who had arrived in their masses; using force to make their presence felt. The rioting upset her dreadfully, but even as a young child as she then was, she wanted to understand.

She said: 'The never-ending errors of judgement, the cruelties of man to fellow man, these things passed me by most of the time; only when they impacted on the small, happy world that my parents tried to make for their children, did I begin to comprehend, but slowly.'

As frightening as the riots were, they did not compare to the awfulness of the bombing of Burma by the Japanese, which started in December 1941.

The attacks forced thousands of Burmese people to leave their country, many of whom – including Pat and her family – sought refuge in India. Burma was 'taken' by the Japanese in March 1942

– its occupation part of the war in the Pacific, which did not end until 15 August 1945, shortly after the Americans dropped two massive atomic bombs on the Japanese towns of Hiroshima and Nagasaki. The end of the war in the Pacific brought about the end of the whole of the Second World War, and also the collapse of the Japanese Empire.

Pat arrived in India in 1942, after a long, exhausting journey by plane, train and boat – that also took her through neighbouring Bangladesh. It was an uncertain, fearful time for Pat, but in some ways exciting, too. She said:

Travel, by this time, had to be seen as an adventure. Each leg of the journey was different, providing at least the opportunity to see dramatically beautiful new parts of the countries we were visiting. We left Chittagong [in Bangladesh] on a night train, which took us to Chandpur, in Assam, from where we boarded a ferry that steamed up the Padma River. This river was so wide in parts that the banks of the river disappeared from sight, it was hard to believe we were not in the open ocean.

Pat also recalled how she 'leant over the railings of the ferry, watching the muddy waters of the river swirl on their way, marvelling at the immensity of this part of India, forgetting for a while that we were homeless'.

Pat was one of hundreds of Burmese who travelled to India this way; but thousands more simply left on foot – not all, of course, could afford transport, so they had to walk; a very long walk it was too, some 600 miles or more, along the notorious 'Burma Road', challenged by monsoons, flooding, freezing temperatures and a lack of food. Long and difficult journeys, such as this, were a feature of war for millions – almost always going to unknown destinations; refugees, lost soldiers, displaced families – walking, escaping, running and collapsing – thousands upon thousands of journeys, each and every one frightening, every step uncertain, never to return to the place they came from.

Returning to the… 'code' (shhhhhh)

We shall now return to the beginning of our chapter; about Pat and Enigma – the mysterious code – the successful translation of which did so much to determine the outcome of the war.

Pat's discovery of this highly secret coding came about because of her employment within the Women's Auxiliary Corps, which she joined after arriving in New Delhi, in the north. She worked in a Special Liaison Unit, firstly as a very junior officer with other young women of her age, meticulously cataloguing endless lists of numbers and letters that were sent through to them from Bletchley Park.

By the time she left in 1944, she had been promoted to Officer rank. It was only then she was informed about the significance of the work she had been doing. Pat said she had very little understanding of her work from the moment she arrived in the unit. Because secrecy was so important, her job wasn't explained to her, she was just told what she had to do. She wasn't even allowed to discuss any aspect of it with the girls she worked with.

It was, quite simply, their job to type the jumble of letters that came through from Bletchley into a machine called a Type-X. The machine would automatically translate the inserted letters into English – revealing the vital messages that would be shared among Commanders at various locations around the Indian coast.

All Pat really knew, she said – especially at the beginning – was that the information was 'very, very hot' and mostly about the movement of Japanese aircraft carriers, and sometimes about the ships that were part of its Imperial Navy, which had been so horribly destructive. Even though Pat wasn't based at Bletchley Park, because of working in connection with its decoding operations, she was able – after the war – to call herself a

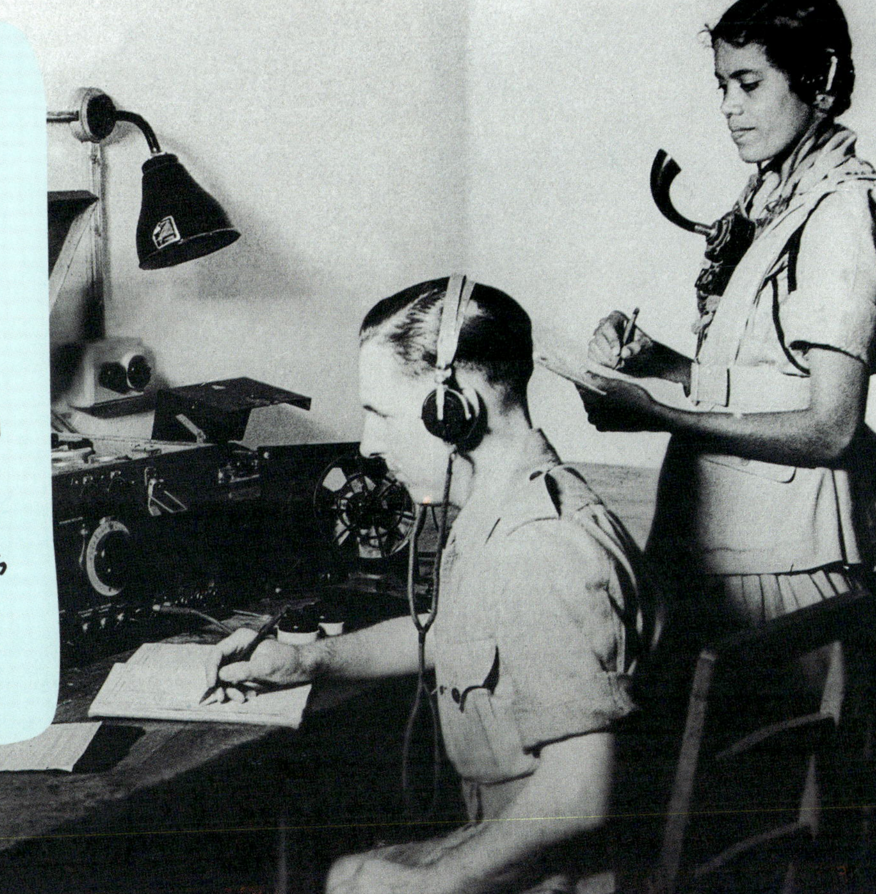

FACT FILE

* The Women's Auxiliary Corps (India) was created in March 1942, out of the Women's Auxiliary Service (Burma).

* By the end of the Second World War, it had recruited 11,500 women.

'Billy Filly', as the women who were part of this operation were known. She is rightly very proud of this! By the end of the war, more than 10,000 people had been part of the Bletchley machine, also known as Britain's 'Ultra Secret', more than three-quarters of whom were women.

Bletchley Park was, undoubtedly, the beating heart of the intelligence operation of the Allies throughout the whole of the war. However, during the war years, its existence remained a closely guarded secret. It pretended to be a large factory, making radios! After all this time, Pat told me she is still amazed at the success of the secrecy, and how those who were part of it managed to keep the secret. She said:

Looking back, it is extraordinary that the secret of all this work was so well kept. But we all learnt how to keep quiet, together, about what we were doing. I think, partly, the war was so frightening it helped you keep quiet _ we weren't even allowed to talk about it with the people we worked with. But we didn't want to discuss it, how awful it would have been to accidentally let something slip that caused terrible consequences. We were all in the same position; we all knew we were just small cogs in a huge wheel _ doing something important but only doing it by force of circumstance. I didn't feel important, thankfully I suppose, none of us did. We just wanted the war to be over. I think if we had felt important, we would have started to talk. And that could have been fatal.

This image shows a room at Bletchley Park, now a museum, decorated as it would have been during World War Two.

Pat also let me into another secret of hers, that Rudyard Kipling's famous poem *If* helped her cope when she found it very difficult not to discuss anything of what she did, with anyone – particularly when she overheard discussions and ideally wanted to tell others not to speak of it too. This is the poem; I am sure Pat would like me to share it with you to help you out in situations that 'drive you crazy' too!

IF

If you can keep your head when all about you
Are losing theirs and blaming it on you,
If you can trust yourself when all men doubt you,
But make allowance for their doubting too;
If you can wait and not be tired by waiting,
Or being lied about, don't deal in lies,
Or being hated, don't give way to hating,
And yet don't look too good, nor talk too wise:
If you can dream—and not make dreams your
	master;
If you can think—and not make thoughts your
	aim;
If you can meet with Triumph and Disaster
And treat those two impostors just the same;
If you can bear to hear the truth you've spoken
Twisted by knaves to make a trap for fools,
Or watch the things you gave your life to, broken,

And stoop and build 'em up with worn-out tools:
If you can make one heap of all your winnings
And risk it on one turn of pitch-and-toss,
And lose, and start again at your beginnings
And never breathe a word about your loss;
If you can force your heart and nerve and sinew
To serve your turn long after they are gone,
And so hold on when there is nothing in you
Except the Will which says to them: 'Hold on!'

If you can talk with crowds and keep your virtue,
Or walk with Kings—nor lose the common touch,
If neither foes nor loving friends can hurt you,
If all men count with you, but none too much;
If you can fill the unforgiving minute
With sixty seconds' worth of distance run,
Yours is the Earth and everything that's in it,
And—which is more—you'll be a Man, my son!

CHAPTER TEN

JOHN OTTEWELL
TO FLY OR NOT TO FLY?

It is a brave young man who leaps off a ten-foot high roof, with an umbrella masquerading as a parachute, in order to experience what it is like to 'fly'. However, as well as brave, it could be argued that such an action is simply foolish; a parachute is made of sheets of silk and usually saves the life of the airman attached to it, because he (or she) has begun their descent to the ground high enough to give the chute time to open – allowing for 'air resistance' to slow the fall.

During the Second World War, standard parachutes issued to British troops measured around 23 feet in diameter when they were fully open. As long as the bale out (meaning to jump with a parachute) began at around 10,000 feet (or above) they had a reasonable chance of landing safely. 'Flight time' with a fully open parachute is around 23 feet per second – so a 10,000-foot drop would have taken around a minute and a half. However, while a parachute might have meant escape from a burning or blown-out aircraft, where, not just how, an airman landed was crucial

too. Thousands fell into enemy territory, alone and vulnerable, and were captured and marched, to prisoner-of-war camps where, unless they made a successful escape attempt, they would have remained until the end of the war.

However, back to the story, and the umbrella that quite simply did not defy gravity in the same way as a parachute would have done, as Flight Lieutenant John Ottewell, explained. John Ottewell was 12 years old when he leapt off a roof at his parent's house, curious to find out what 'flying' was like. Despite a bruising landing and a fierce reprimand, he decided after that that flying was for him and, as soon as he was old enough in 1943, he applied to join the RAF.

A year later, after a testing training regime of drilling and studying, John Ottewell qualified as a navigator and was delighted to learn that his aeroplane was to be the RAF's mightiest, largest aircraft; a four-engine Lancaster bomber. Imagine the noise the four engines, roaring in unison, would have made – each one being more than 1,280 horsepower (hp) (the car your Mum or Dad drives is probably around 100 or 200hp). However, despite its size, it was not invincible, and could not fly quickly enough to outrun an enemy fighter. Its engines, too, were prime targets for enemy guns – it could keep going with two intact, but one was not enough.

The role of navigator was, therefore, extremely important. Operations – particularly over very-heavily defended Germany – were all perilous and all crews would have wanted to reach their targets in the quickest time possible, drop their bombs and return home. It was John Ottewell's job, as holder and keeper of the maps, to guide the pilot to their given destination. Pilot and navigator were two in a crew of seven; they were accompanied by two gunners (rear and mid-upper) and the bomb-aimer, radio operator and flight engineer.

Teamwork was paramount – each had a vital role to play to keep the others safe. Unless they were under attack when communication links might have got broken, they could talk to each other through their comms kit. Sometimes this might have been light-hearted chat to keep their spirits up; but when the enemy was in sight (German 88mm flak guns, for example) targeting them from the ground and in the air, the pilot would have been reliant on the two gunners to tell him what to do, because they were the crew members who could see the enemy approaching… while they too, would have been firing their guns.

Phrases such 'Corkscrew, port, skipper – now!' would have been yelled in instruction to the pilot, and almost certainly a series of rather violent manoeuvres would have begun until, hopefully, the attacker had been shaken off, given up, or run out of fuel and / or ammunition.

When he spoke to me, John Ottewell, was in his early nineties and decades had passed since he had sat in the cockpit. Yet, he was able to describe his experience so vividly that his words put pictures in my head. As he spoke, I felt almost transported to the Lancaster; I felt I was sitting, slightly squashed, maps askew, on a stool facing buttons, levers and knobs on a panel displaying numbers and needle gauges, swinging from left to right… all the time aware of the need to get from A to B via the most direct route, conscious – as was the pilot – that the lives of the other five boys in the aircraft were in their hands. Navigation, as described

by John, was rarely straightforward; on the contrary, because most of their flights were night-flights, finding their way in the darkness in skies busy with the enemy was extremely challenging.

Even with the introduction of radar, which arrived in the early part of the war, intense levels of concentration and attention to detail were continually required. He told me that accuracy was essential in the meeting of objectives on the first occasion as failure could (and sadly did) result in the loss of civilian life, but 'failure' often also meant having to repeat the operation to finish the job. He said: 'We only had our charts, two watches, a compass and a very clever navigational device that enabled the navigator to plot their position by measuring their distance between the stars, called a sextant, to rely on. Not easy given it was usually dark and targets were often camouflaged, or disguised by the use of a clever 'dummy' target nearby. Sometimes I did have to just hope for the best, and even navigate by the stars!' (How much easier, I remember thinking to myself, it must have been on a clear night…).

John also told me, with a twinkle in his eye, 'Even though we had good maps, sometimes we didn't know with any degree of accuracy where anywhere was and sometimes the instruction was to fly somewhere, with even the starting point not well-mapped'. Tricky! Not something we can appreciate today with so many ridiculously easy-to-use satellite navigation kits.

However, not all flights undertaken by Bomber Command involved bombing; many were humanitarian operations – equally vital for the lives they saved. These too were often risky ventures; but journeys I suspect troops were more than willing to undertake because these were the operations that rescued the oppressed and the defeated. John Ottewell told me all about one such operation, which took place in the Netherlands at the end of the war.

Its code-name was Operation *Manna* (manna being the bread of heaven that, in the Bible, God gave to the Israelites during their long years of wandering in the desert). Operation *Manna* was not biblical, of course; it was called this because it involved the delivery of essential, life-saving food to thousands of starving Dutch people, whose supplies had been cut off by the Germans, towards the end of their five-year occupation of Holland. Starvation was a cruel weapon that Germany inflicted upon thousands of people in the Netherlands – especially in the north and the west.

The famine became known as 'Hongerwinter' ('Hunger Winter') and it led to the deaths of 20,000 civilians (mostly elderly men). Thousands more were affected and by

An RAF captain and crew from Bomber Command.

Bomber Command ground crew load food supplies into an Avro Lancaster as part of Operation Manna.

the end of the war 4.5 million Dutch people were dangerously thin and malnourished.

John Ottewell and his crew came to the rescue of some of the dangerously hungry Dutch people by dropping food packages to them, from their aircraft, which was safer than landing the plane on what was still enemy territory. The Germans gave the British very narrow flight paths in which to make their drops; it was vital they stayed within these corridors because to stray out of them would have left them exposed – and very easy targets given they were flying so low. John Ottewell supported this operation as a navigator, on a Lancaster, but how different a flight this was for him, compared to flying over Germany in the darkness, often surrounded by flak.

During Operation *Manna*, he could see the people they were there to defend and care for – and of course they weren't dropping 1,000lb bombs, they were dropping food parcels. He told me that his navigation skills for these flights were absolutely put to the test. He said they dropped their tins of supplies in double sacks, without parachutes, at the designated points, and:

It was difficult, and very important we were precise in those targets, because if we had deviated even slightly off course, we would have found ourselves sitting ducks, flying low and slowly over some of the most well defended areas in Europe. We wouldn't have lived to tell the tale.

But it only took a moment to look down and see the excruciating suffering of those who needed our help. The people were so thin they could have died at any moment. Sometimes they were so desperate for the food parcels they would rush to the designated points, and we would run the risk of hitting them with the tins and sacks.

Some years later, John told me he returned to the Netherlands for a holiday. In a conversation with a local, he mentioned Operation *Manna* and was delighted when his new friend said, 'Yes, I was there too, a child on the ground and very thankful for that food drop, which saved my life!'

Want to learn more? Below is a list of fascinating

PLACES TO VISIT

LONDON

Imperial War Museum London
www.iwm.org.uk/visits/iwm-london

Churchill War Rooms
www.iwm.org.uk/visits/churchill-war-rooms

HMS Belfast
www.iwm.org.uk/visits/hms-belfast

Royal Air Force Museum
www.rafmuseum.org.uk/london

NORTH OF ENGLAND

Fusiliers Museum of Northumberland
www.northumberlandfusiliers.org.uk/visit/

North East Land, Sea & Air Museum
www.nelsam.org.uk

Imperial War Museum North
www.iwm.org.uk/visits/iwm-north

Eden Camp Modern History Museum
www.edencamp.co.uk

SOUTH OF ENGLAND

Bletchley Park
www.bletchleypark.org.uk

The D-Day Story
www.theddaystory.com

Imperial War Museum Duxford
www.iwm.org.uk/visits/iwm-duxford

Fleet Air Arm Museum
www.nmrn.org.uk/visit-us/fleet-air-arm-museum

The Tank Museum
www.tankmuseum.org

SCOTLAND

National Museum of Flight
www.nms.ac.uk/national-museum-of-flight

National War Museum
www.nms.ac.uk/national-war-museum

Military Museum Scotland
www.militarymuseum.scot

WALES

Home Front Museum
www.homefrontmuseum.co.uk

The Royal Welsh Regimental Museum
www.royalwelshmuseum.wales

Royal Welch Fusiliers Museum
www.rwfmuseum.org.uk

NORTHERN IRELAND

Northern Ireland War Memorial Museum
www.niwarmemorial.org

Royal Ulster Rifles Museum
www.royal-irish.com/museums/royal-ulster-rifles-museum